CONTENDERS BIBLE STUDY SERIES™

HOW DO WE KNOW THE BIBLE IS TRUE?

JOHN ANKERBERG
DILLON BURROUGHS

Contenders Bible Study Series

How Do We Know the Bible Is True?

First Printing, May 2008
ISBN 13: 978-089957-779-1

Editing by Rick Steele and Christy Graeber

Layout by PerfecType, Nashville, Tennessee

Cover Design by Indoor Graphics Corp., Chattanooga, Tennessee

Printed in Canada
13 12 11 10 09 08 –T– 6 5 4 3 2 1

Table of Contents

Foreword

By Dr. Norman Geisler

When Jude wrote his New Testament letter to Christians in the early church he felt compelled to urge his readers to "contend for the faith" (Jude 1:3). His words continue to provide a strong motivation for us today to understand the reasons behind what we believe both for our own personal growth and in order to communicate our faith to others.

The Contenders series of Bible study books by John Ankerberg and Dillon Burroughs is designed to provide a response for this tremendous need. As followers of Christ, we are instructed to be prepared to share the reason for our hope (1 Peter 3:15). In addition, those still seeking the truth regarding Jesus and the Word of God are encouraged, as the hearers of Paul in Berea were, to examine the Scriptures to discover if what they had been taught was true (Acts 17:11).

The innovative material found in this series can assist you in two specific ways. First, if you are already a believer in Christ, this series can provide answers to many of the complex questions you may be facing—or that you are asking yourself. Second, if you are a skeptic or seeker of spiritual truth contemplating what it means to follow Jesus Christ, this series can also help provide a factual basis for the Christian faith and the questions in your quest. You can feel free to wrestle with the difficult issues of the Christian faith in the context of friendly conversation with others. This is a powerful tool for individuals who sincerely desire to learn more about God and the amazing truths given to us in the Bible.

If you are one of the people who have chosen to participate in this new series, I applaud your efforts to grow in spiritual truth. Let the pages of this resource provide the basis for your journey as you learn more about contending for the faith we communicate in Jesus Christ.

Dr. Norman Geisler,
co-founder of Southern Evangelical Seminary
and author of seventy books, including the award-winning
Baker Encyclopedia of Christian Apologetics

Introduction

Welcome to the Contenders series! This small-group curriculum was developed with the conviction that claims about today's spiritual issues can and should be investigated. Christianity, sometimes stereotyped as non-intellectual and uneducated, is not allowed to make assertions of faith without providing practical answers why it should be taken seriously. If the Bible claims to be God's Word and claims to provide explanations for the most significant issues of life, both now and eternally, these assertions should be carefully examined. If this investigation proves these beliefs flawed, the only reasonable choice is to refuse to follow the Christian Scriptures as truth. However, if our investigation of the evidence leads to the discovery of truth, then the search will have been worthwhile. In fact, it will be life-changing.

Christians understand that God welcomes sincere seekers of truth. In fact, Jesus Christ Himself openly cheered such inquiry. The Bible is not a book shrouded in mystery, open to only a select group of experts. It is widely available for discussion and learning by anyone. The core beliefs of Christianity are publicly presented to anyone willing to consider their truths, whether skeptic, seeker, or life-long believer.

Consider this book your invitation. Investigate the choices, analyze the beliefs, and make your decisions. But be prepared—the truth you encounter is not another file to simply add to your collection. The truth of God's Word will transform every area of your life.

We often learn that we have mistakenly believed something that turns out to be false. We may even find ourselves not wanting to accept truth because it infringes upon our lifestyle or conflicts with long-held personal values. Through this series of discussion questions we will journey together to answer the question Pilate asked Jesus long ago: "What is truth?" (John 18:38). As authors, it is our hope that you will ultimately come to realize that Christian faith is based upon solid evidence worthy to build one's life upon. Whether you are currently still building your opinions on spiritual issues or are already a follower of Christ developing answers for your own questions and the questions of others, these guides will assist you on a captivating exploration of spiritual issues necessary in order to "contend for the faith" (Jude 3).

The Contenders Series for Your Group

The Contenders series is purposely designed to give truth seekers (those still investigating a relationship with Christ) an opportunity to ask questions and probe into the basics of Christianity within the friendly, caring environment of small-group discussion—typically in a group no larger than about a dozen people, with one or two individuals who serve as the discussion leaders. These leaders are responsible to coordinate the regular gatherings, build relationships with group members, and prepare to ask and answer questions, involving each person in the discussion. Through a combination of caring friendships, intelligent conversations, and genuine spiritual interest, it is our hope that these discussions will provide the basis for a fresh approach to exploring key concepts of Christian belief.

Because one of the intentions of this series is to address the real questions of the spiritual seeker, the questions are presented to represent the viewpoints of both the Christian and the skeptic. While the truths of Christianity are explicitly affirmed, hopefully many who join these discussions will find their own viewpoints understood and represented along the way. As seekers and skeptics feel valued in their current beliefs, they will be more open to honest discussion that leads to truth. The ultimate hope behind the Contenders series is that many who are seeking will come to know the truth about Christ, and that those who already follow Jesus will understand how to address the issues of their friends who are still exploring Christianity.

Of course, it is also important that those who already follow Jesus learn to grow in the basic beliefs of the Christian faith. As they do so, it will become easier to communicate the good news of the Christian faith in normal, everyday conversations with co-workers, neighbors, classmates, relatives, and even complete strangers. The process of struggling through these important issues and difficult questions will not only enhance one's own personal growth but also provide many specific details that can be used in everyday scenarios when the topic of faith arises with others.

Many groups will consist of some blend of believers and seekers. For example, your church may use this material for one of its small groups that consists mostly of people who already follow Christ. However, in the process, group members should feel comfortable and even encouraged to invite friends who have yet to begin a relationship with Christ. Special events designed to invite friends from outside of your current group, including simple social opportunities like dinner parties, a game night, movie night, or other activity should be considered. Regardless of the specific options selected, we pray that you will benefit tremendously as you use these guides to connect through interactive discussions about the issues of ultimate importance.

How to Use This Guide

Getting Started

At the start of each session is a segment of introductory material, typically several paragraphs in length. Each participant will want to read this information before the session begins, even if it is read again when the group is together. This "Getting Started" section is written with the skeptic in mind, often including very controversial perspectives to stimulate challenging discussion. As a result, each person should instantly feel the ability to share his or her viewpoint within the safe context of a caring group of friends.

Talk about It

Next, each session includes a range of ten to twenty questions your group can use during discussion. Most groups will find it impossible to use every single question every time. The options are either to choose which questions best fit the needs of your group, or to use the questions for more than one time together. The key component of this "Talk about It" section is to include each and every person, allowing the conversation to help people process their thoughts on the issue.

Often, the opening question of each session is a simple opinion question. Through the use of this ice-breaker approach, the conversation quickly takes off as each person offers his or her thoughts on a non-threatening issue that touches on the topic of the particular session. Certainly, the creativity of the group may also provide additional or alternative ice-breaker questions or activities to start each session. The goal is to achieve quick and enjoyable involvement by everyone in the group.

Here's What I'm Thinking

The next section, called "Here's What I'm Thinking," transitions the time of discussion toward a more emotional element. The questions in this section deal directly with personal responses to the material in each session rather than just intellectual facts or opinions. This is a time to communicate what each person is feeling about the topic, since this is a critical step in helping a person come to a personal decision about the issue.

What Now?

In the "What Now?" section, participants are challenged to move beyond both intellectual and emotional responses toward personal application of the material shared in the session. Once each person has considered his or her personal position on the issue, the next part of the process is to determine how this position influences daily living. One interesting impact of this section is that each person will begin to understand the implications of both true and faulty beliefs, along with charting personal changes in belief formation from one session to the next.

Consider This

Each session also includes one or more segments called "Consider This," designed to provide additional factual material appropriate to each discussion. Each "Consider This" section is immediately followed by a question based on the material, so it's important (especially for leaders) to read and understand this part before each meeting.

What Others Have Said

Throughout each session, participants will discover various quotes on the topic of discussion. Rather than quoting primarily academic sources, these quotes provide diverse perspectives from those critical of the Christian faith and well-known personalities from today's culture, along with well-worded thoughts from some of today's top writers.

Additional Resources

At the end of each guide, we have provided a list of several resources from the authors on the issue. This is only an introduction to a vast array of print, audio, video, and electronic materials based on decades of research in these areas.

A Word to Discussion Leaders

One distinctive feature of the Contenders series is that the learning does not end with the material found in this book. The series website www.contendersseries.com is loaded with interactive links to numerous online articles, outside internet links, video clips, audio responses, and creative ways to help direct the discussions in your group. We hope you'll also find it to be an excellent personal study source as well. And if you still don't find the answer you're looking for, or just want to connect with the authors of this resource, you'll find a place where you can email your questions and other feedback for personal responses.

Creating Boundaries

These guides consist mostly of questions for one reason—they are intended to spark conversation rather than fill-in-the-blank answers. In one sense, these discussions are not conventional Bible studies, though they often refer to Bible verses and biblical themes. Instead, consider these sessions as study guides, designed to assist participants in discussing what they feel and think on important spiritual issues.

Each topic is developed around a central point and clear conclusion, but they leave much of the "middle" open to the thoughts of those involved in the discussion. Every person brings perspectives, past experiences, and personal questions to the group. Rather than suppress these individual contributions, each session seeks to draw out the thoughts of each person, comparing the thinking of those in the group with what the Bible communicates in order to point members toward spiritual growth.

Much of the group's success will be determined by its leader(s). Those coordinating the group can also find additional material for each session at the Contenders series website at www.contendersseries.com. At the website, leader(s) will find suggested articles, additional facts, and suggested answers for many of the questions in each session. (Individual participants in your group are welcome to use these resources as well.) In addition, a personal daily study in the AMG Following God™ series called *Defending Your Faith* is available for those who desire a more in-depth study that can be used in combination or separately from these group guides.

In addition, you may want to keep the following list of suggestions in mind as you prepare to participate in your group discussions.[1]

1. The Contenders series does not require that the topics be discussed in an exact order. The guides, in addition to the topics within each guide, can be utilized in any order or even independently of each other, based on the needs of your group or class.

2. It is important to read over the material before each meeting (especially for leaders). The more familiar you are with the topic, the better your ability to discuss the issue during the actual group experience.

3. Actively participate in group discussion. The leader of this group is not expected to share a lecture, but to encourage each person to share in dialogue. This includes both points of agreement and disagreement.

Plan to share your beliefs openly and honestly.

4. Be sensitive to other people in the group. Listen attentively when others share and affirm whenever possible. It is important to show respect for the opinions of others even if they don't agree with your position. However, it is likewise important to affirm the biblical truths of each topic in wrapping up each area of discussion.

5. Be careful not to dominate the conversation. Feel free to share, but be sensitive to the length of time that you share in relation to the input of others in the group.

6. Stay focused on the discussion topic. Discussion can easily digress into side topics that may be equally important, but are unrelated to the session in discussion. As a leader, feel free to say: "That's a good issue to discuss. We should talk about that more sometime, but we need to get back to the topic for this session."

7. Encourage group participants to bring a Bible with them. While we believe there is no "perfect" Bible translation, we believe it is important to be sensitive to the needs of seekers and newer believers in your group by at least including a contemporary translation such as the New International Version or New Living Translation that can help provide quick understanding of Bible passages. Many good study Bibles with helpful notes are also available today to help group members in their growth. In these guides, the New International Version has been used unless otherwise noted.

8. Invest some extra time reading in the Bible, other

recommended resources, or related audio and video content as you work through these sessions. The "Additional Resources" section at the back of each guide provides several such resources to enhance your growth.

The Greatest of These Is Love

Christianity is all about Christ. The very Son of God left the glory of heaven, was born of a woman, lived among ordinary people like you and me, and died a horrific death, before His resurrection and ascension back to heaven. Shortly before His death, He shared with His followers, "Greater love has no man than this, that he lay down his life for his friends" (John 15:13). Jesus provided a perfect example of this love by offering His life for us. As the apostle Paul later wrote, "Now these three remain: faith, hope, and love. But the greatest of these is love" (1 Corinthians 13:13).

As we learn to "contend for the faith," it is of utmost importance that we live with this same overwhelming love to those we encounter. The Christian faith provides more than ample evidence for the hope that we have in Christ. We invite you to explore these life-changing truths with others in a small-group context that leads to even further growth in your spiritual journey. May God bless you as you pursue the truth of Christ and "contend for the faith."

Setting the Stage: How Do We Know the Bible Is True?

Muhammad taught that he had received the very words of Allah through a series of revelations from the angel Gabriel. These revelations were later compiled into the Qu'ran, forming the sacred book of Islam. For a Muslim to even question the accuracy of the Qu'ran is a serious sin. In fact, even today, the legal system of several nations is baed solely on the Qu'ran.

Jehovah's Witnesses believe in a sacred book, too. They have a "Bible," which they believe has now been properly re-translated by the movement's leaders. The *Book of Mormon* contains Joseph Smith's new translation of the materials he claimed were revealed to him by the angel Moroni. Kabbalah has the *Zohar*. Hinduism has the *Vedas*. Buddhism has the *Four Noble Truths* and *The Eightfold Path*.

Who's to say which books are really from God? Couldn't these holy books all be coming from the same place? What makes the Bible special? A Mormon, Muslim, Jehovah's Witness, Hindu, or Buddhist would each claim his or her scriptures are "the" truth. But can they all be right if their beliefs contradict each other? How can a person know the truth?

Some argue that a claim to have had an experience with God or a supernatural encounter settles the issue, but others believe this is not enough. Religious literature, like any other documents making claims of importance, should be examined before their teachings are accepted. Any inaccuracies, whether in historical facts or authorship, should show us that the book can't be trusted in spiritual areas, either.

Many people have completely given up separating what is true from what is untrue. An attitude of, "What you believe is true is true for you," or "Whatever works for you," has taken the place of sincere effort to evaluate truth. Others are even more critical. Consider the following evaluation from Athiests.org:

> The Christian faith is based on the belief that the Bible is indeed the word of god. If the Bible cannot be shown to be inspired, then the Christian faith could be said to be false and no more than a farce. If the Bible cannot be shown to be inspired, then Christianity can be said to be the same as any other religion that has been devised and practiced by man.[2]

What evidence is there that the Bible is any more special than any other spiritual book? Does it contain any information that should cause us to take it more serious than say, the Qu'ran? Or do the Bible's teachings simply serve as a crutch for weak-willed people, as some claim?

These questions are not to be taken lightly. The issue at stake is whether or not an all-powerful God has communicated to humanity through a written message, and where that message can be discovered. As one philosopher has said, "If that book exists, it is the most valuable book in the world."

Maybe God hasn't spoken at all. That's the view of the atheist. However, as limited human beings, there is no way to "prove" for certain that God has *not* spoken. On the other side, if God *has* spoken, then those words should be evident and treated with extreme care and importance. But to determine whether God has spoken and where His words are to be found requires sincere investigation. This series of discussions will help you investigate the answer to the question, "How do we know the Bible is true?" so you can determine what you personally believe on this critical issue.

SESSION 1:

How Did We Get the Bible?

Getting Started

In the history of the English language, there have been more than 450 translations of the Bible. When you walk into a bookstore today to find a Bible, you can choose from every assorted color, style, translation, study format, and binding, including magazine-style versions and even a "duct-tape" Bible.

Christians claim that the Bible is "God's Word," the very words of God revealed to people. Even so, few of the people who claim to be Christians have any idea of where the Bible came from or how the Bible ended up in the form we have today. Most people would agree that God didn't simply fax or email the text to a publisher for printing, but somebody wrote it down. Who was it? Where and when did it happen? How do we know they really heard from God when they wrote it?

If you were to read the Bible for the first time with no prior knowledge of its contents, how do you think you would understand it? Would it fascinate you or frustrate you? Would you consider it sacred writing or just another book?

One of the top observations made by people who examine the contents of the Bible, whether at the academic level or among friends over a cup of coffee, is the human aspect of the writings. When we talk about the Bible as "God's Word" we sometimes give the impression that God actually wrote down the very words outside of human influence. There would be commands and lists of dos and donts, but little about individual personalities.

Yet the Bible begins with the words, "In the beginning God created the heavens and the earth." God isn't even speaking in the first person. The words are written from the perspective of a human author rather than a holy deity. As we read across the vast pages of Scripture, we discover that the text is communicated as a combination of "God says" and the accounts of various people who represent Him at different points in history.

Then there's the issue of how to interpret the Bible. Some of its teachings are difficult to understand. Are these symbolic, or should they be taken literally? Did God whisper the words in the ears of the person writing each book or did they just feel "inspired" and jot down their thoughts? How can we tell the difference? In what ways were God's impressions to them any different or any better than what God speaks to us today?

When it comes down to it, how did we get the Bible? Who selected the table of contents we have today? Did they leave out any missing gospels or include something that is inaccurate? What if writers sincerely thought they heard from God but were just writing their own thoughts? The origin of the Bible seems more like an unsolved mystery than a holy book. If the Bible is really God's Word for the world, then these are some questions that really need answers.

Talk about It

1. What were you taught (if anything) about the Bible when you were a child? What did you think about the Bible's stories at that time?

2. What are some of the questions you continue to have regarding the Bible now? If you could have any one issue about the Bible answered for you in this group, what would it be?

Here's What I'm Thinking

Surprises from God

If God wanted to write a book for us to read, don't you think He would just dictate to someone what to write in His book? That would seem to make the most sense from our perspective. Muslims had one prophet—Muhammad—to take down the exact words of Allah given through an angel for their holy book, the Qu'ran. A newcomer to Christianity would probably expect something similar.

Yet the Bible is full of surprises. Large portions include historical records from people who lived during a particular time. Several chapters are nothing but lists of family history—Adam became the father of Seth, and Seth became the father of . . . and on and on. There are lots of strange names for people and places, in addition to details of historical events that don't seem very relevant for today. Sure, there are also several places where prophets, apostles, or other holy people speak for

God, but the lives of these individuals are often marred with their own failures or have a past that simply isn't mentioned.

In the New Testament accounts of Jesus, we are told about many of His teachings and miracles. These books include much more than just transcripts of his sermons. Later writers like Peter, Paul, and John spend more time talking about themselves and their current audience than they do quoting the words of their founder. There may be some words of God in the Bible, but how do we know the Bible is "God's Word" in its entirety?

Quick Facts About the Bible			
	Chapters	**Verses**	**Words**
Old Testament	929	23,138	602,582
New Testament	260	7,957	169,751*

*These statistics based on the King James Version[3]

3. Why would a perfect God author a book full of history, family records, and stories of His followers making mistakes? How does this make it a more accurate book?

4. When biblical writers talk about themselves or the people surrounding them, how does this add significance to the Bible?

Who Are the People Who Helped Write the Bible?

Those unfamiliar with the Bible often do not realize that the Bible, in one sense, is not a single book, but rather a collection of sixty-six books. Yet there is a central message that remains consistent throughout its pages that continues to point toward one holy God who shows love to his world through the life of his Son Jesus. The sixty-six books of the Bible were. . .

- written by over forty people.
- over a 1,400 year period.
- on three continents (Asia, Africa, and Europe).
- in three languages (Hebrew, Aramaic, and Greek).
- in multiple genres (history, poetry, prophecy, narrative).
- by people of diverse backgrounds (priests, a doctor, political leaders, teachers, fishermen, shepherds).

5. What could be some disadvantages of including so many diverse people in compiling the Bible? How could this diversity be viewed as an advantage in showing that the Bible is God's Word?

What Makes the Bible Unique?

The Bible's human writers never claimed to be superheroes, yet stressed that they were used by God to write down His words. They noted that they were accurate in their use of history, included eyewitness testimonies, used accurate sources, and claimed that their predictions would be fulfilled.

➢ *Historical Accuracy*

Therefore, since I myself have carefully investigated everything from the beginning, it seemed good also to me to write an orderly account for you, most excellent Theophilus, so that you may know the certainty of the things you have been taught. (Luke 1:3–4)

Jesus did many other miraculous signs in the presence of his disciples, which are not recorded in this book. But these are written that you may believe that Jesus is the Christ, the Son of God, and that by believing you may have life in his name. (John 20:30–31)

➢ *Eyewitness Accuracy*

As Jesus went on from there, he saw a man named Matthew sitting at the tax collector's booth. "Follow me," he told him, and Matthew got up and followed him. (Matthew 9:9) [Matthew wrote this account about himself.]

We did not follow cleverly invented stories when we told you about the power and coming of our Lord Jesus Christ, but we were ***eyewitnesses*** *of his majesty.* (2 Peter 1:16)

That which was from the beginning, which we have heard, which we have seen with our eyes, which we have looked at and our hands have touched—this we proclaim concerning the Word of life. (1 John 1:1)

➢ *Prophetic Accuracy*

Therefore I told you these things long ago; before they happened I announced them to you. (Isaiah 48:5)

All this took place to fulfill what the Lord had said through the prophet. (Matthew 1:22)

6. Anyone can claim to speak for God, but not just anyone can prove it. What kind of proof would you need to show you that the words of the Bible are from God?

Who Chose the Books of the Bible?

The Bible consists of two major sections: the Old Testament and the New Testament. The Old Testament contains thirty-nine books (22 in the Hebrew Bible due to how some of the books were combined, though the content is the same). The last book of the Old Testament was completed by 400 BC, and many of the books were considered God's Word long before this time (especially the Books of Moses used as the Jewish law).

In AD 90 in Jamnia, a group of Jewish scholars gathered to confirm which books were to be considered part of their collection of scriptures. The Old Testament had been translated into Greek long before the time of Jesus, so we know that these books had been in use long before this meeting. This is simply the earliest known list that includes our present day Old Testament table of contents.

In addition, Jesus Himself supported this list of Old Testament books through His teachings. In Matthew 23:35, Jesus mentioned the murders of Abel (in Genesis) and Zechariah (from the end of the Old Testament period) as start and end points of Old Testament revelation. His teaching in the Sermon on the Mount in Matthew 5:17 also noted that Jesus came to fulfill the Law (Genesis through Deuteronomy) and the Prophets (a major portion of the Old Testament).

A further evidence of the support of the New Testament writers of the Old Testament Scriptures is their frequent quotes from and allusions to these books. In fact, thirty-two percent of the New Testament's verses include material used from the Old Testament.

The New Testament consists of twenty-seven books that were all written between about AD 40 and 96. They were immediately circulated in the earliest churches and quoted by early church writers even before the end of the first century. For instance, Irenaeus (AD 170) quoted twenty-three of the twenty-seven New Testament books less than one hundred years after the writing of the New Testament books. This means he must have had access to this many books within a generation of the apostles. This would have been a tremendous accomplishment for a culture whose writings could only be spread through handwritten copies!

Collections of these books remain from as early as the second century, with our earliest complete New Testaments from the fourth century. The earliest list that includes the twenty-seven books we use today was written in AD 367 by Athanasius. New Testament Greek scholar Dr. Kurt Aland comments that the New Testament, ". . . was not imposed from the top, be it by bishops or synods, and then accepted by the communities. . . . The organized church did not create the canon [New Testament]; it recognized the canon that had been created."[4]

That is an important statement. The early Christians, like the Jews before them, recognized the claim of books from

God. But on what basis were the books of the New Testament selected? The following questions guided the recognition of which books were from God:[5]

- ***Was the book written or supported by a prophet or apostle of God?*** This was the single most important factor. The reasoning here is that the Word of God which is inspired by the Spirit of God for the people of God must be communicated through a person of God. Second Peter 1:20–21 assures us that Scripture is only written by God's people. In Galatians 1:1–24, the apostle Paul argued support for the Book of Galatians by appealing to the fact that he was an authorized messenger of God, an apostle.
- ***Is the book authoritative?*** In other words, can it be said of the book as it was said of Jesus, "The people were amazed at his teaching, because he taught them as one who had authority, not as the teachers of the law" (Mark 1:22)? Put another way, does the book ring with the sense of, "The Lord says. . . ."?
- ***Does the book tell the truth about God consistent with previous revelation?*** The Bereans searched the Old Testament Scriptures to determine whether Paul's teaching was true (Acts 17:11). They knew that if Paul's teaching did not resonate with the Old Testament writings, it could not be of God. Agreement with all earlier revelation was essential (Galatians 1:8).
- ***Does the book give evidence of having the power of God?*** Any writing that does not exhibit the transforming power of God in the lives of its readers could not have come from God. Scripture says that the Word of God is "living and active" (Hebrews 4:12). Second Timothy 3:16–17 indicates that God's

Word has a transforming effect. If the book in question did not have the power to change a life, then the book could not have come from God.

- ***Was the book accepted by the people of God?*** In Old Testament times, Moses' scrolls were immediately placed into the Ark of the Covenant (Deuteronomy 31:24–26), as were Joshua's (Joshua 24:26). In the New Testament, Paul thanked the Thessalonians for receiving his message as the Word of God (1 Thessalonians 2:13). Paul's letters were also circulated among the churches (Colossians 4:16; 1 Thessalonians 5:27). It was common that God's people would accept God's Word as such from the start.

7. In what ways could the slow process of confirming the books of the New Testament strengthen the case that the books chosen were correct?

8. Today, we continue to hear of so-called lost gospels or missing gospels. How should we respond to such claims? How do you think the apostles and early church leaders would have responded to this question?

This Is Only a Test

The Scriptures themselves provide a test to determine whether the message of a person who claimed to be a prophet was true. In the Old Testament, two tests were given regarding messages that claimed to be from God.

First, the prophet's message had to be one hundred percent accurate:

> *You may say to yourselves, "How can we know when a message has not been spoken by the* Lord*?" If what a prophet proclaims in the name of the* Lord *does not take place or come true, that is a message the* Lord *has not spoken. That prophet has spoken presumptuously. Do not be afraid of him.* (Deuteronomy 18:21–22)

If a person spoke for God, their predictions had to be perfect, with no room for error.

Second, the person who spoke for God had to be consistent with the rest of the inspired words of God:

> *If a prophet, or one who foretells by dreams, appears among you and announces to you a miraculous sign or wonder, and if the sign or wonder of which he has spoken takes place, and he says, "Let us follow other gods" (gods you have not known) "and let us worship them," you must not listen to the words of that prophet or dreamer.* (Deuteronomy 13:1–2)

The Old Testament refused to even accept a person who could accurately predict the future if the person taught other to follow different gods.

In the New Testament, this same general principle was followed:

> *. . . do not treat prophecies with contempt. Test everything. Hold on to the good. Avoid every kind of evil.* (1 Thessalonians 5:20–21)

Prophecies were not to be treated lightly, but were rather to be examined. Those teachings that were consistent with the rest of the God's known words were to be followed ("the good"). False teachings or anything evil was to be avoided. This advice is found again later in Paul's warning to Timothy to, ". . . command certain men not to teach false doctrines any longer nor to devote themselves to myths and endless genealogies" (1 Timothy 1:3–4).

9. Some people today claim to be prophets, yet are accurate only a very small portion of the time. Would such people pass the tests given in the Bible? How would such a test rate past religious thinkers and leaders, such as Edgar Cayce or Joseph Smith (founder of Mormonism), or the early leaders of the Jehovah's Witnesses, who each made prophecies that did not come true?

Prophetic Leader	Inaccurate Prophecy
Jehovah's Witnesses founder Charles T. Russell	"All present governments will be overthrown and dissolved" in 1914[6]
Edgar Cayce	Predicted that California would fall into the Pacific Ocean in the 1970s.[7]
Jeane Dixon	Predicted that World War III would begin in 1958.[8]

10. If a church leader today could accurately foretell the future, yet taught people to worship multiple gods, how should this person be treated according to the Bible verses we just read?

What Now?

11. Why do many people struggle to accept the Bible as the only written authority from God that is unique and better than any other spiritual writing? In what ways do you struggle personally with this issue?

12. What evidence would it take to persuade you that the Bible is God's truth and should be treated as the authoritative spiritual guide for your life?

13. How has your view of the Bible influenced the way you have treated the Bible (in terms of attitude or personal study of it)?

Consider This

This session is the start of an investigation of the claims of the Bible as God's Word. You are not expected to have all of the right answers. The only expectation is to have an open viewpoint and a desire to learn. In fact, you are probably involved in this group right now due to your curiosity to discover answers regarding some of your own doubts, or at least the doubts of others in your life. Rather than pretending to have the issues all figured out, feel free to express some of your difficult questions and concerns as you continue with this group. The only way to find the answers to your questions is to ask the real questions that still exist in your own mind.

To help identify ways your viewpoints or beliefs are growing during these sessions, throughout this series you will have moments to express where you currently stand on this journey. As you continue to learn, you may find some of your opinions changing from one session to the next. The key idea to remember is that this is a time of growth rather than a test. The more time you invest seeking the truth regarding God's Word, the better your understanding will become on the issues discussed in this guide.

14. Which of the following statements best describes your personal perspective regarding the Bible? (Circle all that apply.)

    A. The Bible is irrelevant for my life.
    B. The Bible is an interesting book, but I'm not sure it's perfect.
    C. The Bible is no different from any other sacred writing.
    D. The Bible contains some truth, but I don't believe it is "God's Word."
    E. The Bible is God's word to humanity, given without error.
    F. Other thoughts:

SESSION 2

Isn't the Bible Full of Myths and Legends?

Getting Started

Fiction makes for popular reading in our culture. Whether the latest thriller by Tom Clancy or Vince Flynn, the mysteries of James Patterson, the escapades of young Harry Potter, or the romantic adventures found in Janet Evanovich's titles, millions of faithful fans read into the early morning hours to discover how the twists and turns of their latest saga will unfold.

Some claim that the Bible should line the same row in bookstores as some of their favorite novels. Isn't it the same? It's full of wonderful stories and adventures, but there's no way all of those supernatural events really happened. Those who do attempt to read the Bible literally find themselves stumped trying to explain countless conflicts and factual errors that have no reasonable solution. In the end, those who try to prove the Bible is completely true find themselves looking ridiculous. You might as well try to prove that *Romeo and Juliet* is a true historical account.

A talking snake in a garden? A person walking on water? People walking through a sea on dry land? People coming back to life from the dead days later? Centuries ago, people were gullible enough to believe those tales, but any intelligent reader today knows such accounts never took place, right?

Those who believe the Bible is full of legendary stories sometimes dismiss the Bible completely. Their thinking is that, "If the Bible is full of fairy tales, then why bother? Let little kids read it at bedtime, but keep it away from me." In their eyes, Santa Claus, the Easter Bunny, UFOs, and David and Goliath all stand at the same level. Let people believe what they want, but leave me out of it.

Most people, however, take a more moderate approach to the Bible's accounts. The prevailing sentiment is that the Bible makes some outlandish claims, yet there are many good morals to be learned from reading it. Many appreciate it, but just don't take it too seriously. They think they'll get more out of it that way and not be bothered by attempting to explain the parts that don't make sense. It's been said that Thomas Jefferson had a Bible to which he took scissors and cut out the parts he didn't like or believe. What if he had the right idea? Keep the parts we like and leave out the rest.

While the first approach may strike us as more negative than the other, both views simply seek to avoid dealing with the Bible as a work of nonfiction or a book that is historically accurate. Yet many Christians believe there is a third option that makes much more sense. Christians believe that if God really led his followers to write the information we find in the Bible, then this information must be true and not simply made up of myths or legends. If they are right about this than maybe Moses really did part the waters with his walking stick; Jesus really did make a blind man see and Elijah really did call down fire from heaven. In their worldview, the Bible is to be taken very seriously, because it is sacred revelation directly from God.

Is this literalist approach in the areas of history, miracles, and theology the one the Bible itself claims we should take?

Does the person who believes the Bible is accurate have any evidence to support such a position? Can the Bible possibly be a factual book without myth? Time to begin the discussion!

Talk about It

1. What is one of your favorite childhood stories? Why do people love telling and hearing these kinds of stories even if they are not true?

2. If you were read Bible stories as a child, what did you think about them at the time? Did they seem real, or were they told just like other stories from your childhood?

3. What are some of the accounts in the Bible that are often regarded as myths? Why are these particular ones selected?

Here's What I'm Thinking

The Meanings of Myths

The word "myth" comes from the Greek word *mythos*, which means "story." In ancient Greek culture, the belief in myths was originally taken for granted. However, over time, some began to question the truth of the accounts of gods and goddesses from the distant past. Over time, Greek myth transitioned from an accepted part of culture to stories that contained important lessons for life as well as entertainment for the people, similar in many ways to how films are used today.

Other myths are built upon historical events that have been exaggerated over long periods of time. These include Western accounts such as Robin Hood, the Knights of King Arthur, and the stories of Saint Patrick. Each was based on a historical situation that was true, but has become layered throughout the centuries with legendary additions that cloud what really took place.

There are people today who suggest that Christianity has become shrouded in religious mythology in a similar way. In other words, there is some truth to the stories recorded in the Bible, but the "true" portions of these accounts have grown and expanded over time to the point that we cannot even tell what really happened. Tales of a six-day creation, a snake in a garden, a worldwide flood, and superheroes like Samson are the result of multiple retellings of stories that have grown and expanded over centuries of tradition. Other religions include their own mythology, such as the Native American religions, Eastern religions with their tales of reincarnation, or accounts of Muhammad's ascent to heaven. Christianity is just another of the same, isn't it?

4. When people speak of the Bible as full of myths and legends, what type of legends do you think they have in mind?

5. What are some of the ways you think the accounts of the Bible are distinctly different from childhood tales like "Sleeping Beauty?"

Fact or Fiction?

Reference works (such as Encarta online and major print encyclopedias), often include the following biblical accounts as mythological:

- The Genesis account of creation
- The long lives of early humans (some over 900 years!)
- Noah and the ark
- Abraham talking with God and angels
- Jacob wrestling with God
- The ten plagues of Egypt
- The parting of the Red Sea
- The Israelites eating manna in the desert for forty years
- The walls of Jericho falling down
- The sun standing still
- Samson killing hundreds of people at a time
- David killing a nine-foot, nine-inch Goliath
- Jonah and the great fish
- Shadrach, Meshach, and Abednego walking out of the fiery furnace
- Daniel surviving the lion's den
- Jesus born of a virgin
- Jesus healing the sick and casting out demons
- Jesus coming alive three days after death

Skeptics claim that rather than attempting to explain these and other Bible miracles, it would be better to simply accept that they are legendary and not literal accounts. Such reasoning allows us to appreciate the Bible's literary beauty without accepting all of its contents as accurate or inspired.

While this may make sense to some, we should pause and seriously consider that the Bible itself claims to be the very Word of God. This claim is clearly seen in places like 2 Timothy 3:15–17, where Paul writes, "From infancy you have known the holy Scriptures, which are able to make you wise for salvation through faith in Christ Jesus. *All Scripture* is God-breathed and is useful for teaching, rebuking, correcting and training in righteousness, so that the man of God may be thoroughly equipped for every good work" (emphasis added).

Here, the Bible states four specific beliefs about its content. First, it calls itself *holy Scripture*. This indicates that the Bible believes itself to be a special book of greater importance than all other writings. Second, it claims to *make its readers wise*. Third, it claims to be *God-breathed*, a reference to the Bible as coming directly from God Himself. Because God reveals himself as perfect and true (and as someone who cannot lie), His words are also to be accepted as accurate and without error. Fourth, the Bible claims it is *useful*. Useful in this context means that it prepares the follower of Christ to live out His teachings.

This brings us back around to where we began: is the Bible completely true in all it states or is it merely a human book? While it is written by humans, it is either "of God" or it is not. It can't be both.

6. How should we decide which parts of the Bible are intended to be taken literally and which parts are not?

7. How often do you think Christians actually investigate the stories they read in the Bible to discover if they are based on historical facts? Why do you think so many people accept what they read in the Bible without investigating if for themselves?

8. How can personal bias (such as believing miracles do not happen) get in the way of investigating the accuracy of the Bible?

9. Do you think the evidence generally used to question the Bible's accuracy is convincing, or is it often based on an emotional response? In what ways have you experienced this in people you have talked with regarding Christianity?

Over 200 Flood Stories?

Did you know that there are over two hundred stories worldwide of a large-scale flood that destroyed the majority of people and animals? One of the most famous extra-biblical accounts is the *The Gilgamesh Epic*. It is an epic poem from Babylonia from the seventh century BC that speaks of a man who constructed a large boat to escape a major flood. In the Gilgamesh version, the ship was a large cube that could roll in the high floodwaters. While it is very different than the story of Noah's Ark in Genesis 6–9, it notes: 1) a massive flood, 2) a man who built a ship ahead of time to escape the flood, 3) a family that escaped with him, 4) a mass destruction of animal and human life, and 5) a new start through the surviving family. While legend has certainly emerged in various forms over the centuries, these legends support the assertions that a great flood did take place. Christians believe the Genesis flood account is the accurate version of this event.

10. In what ways does the existence of many other flood stories suggest the probability of a real historical event?

11. Jesus referred to many miraculous accounts from the Old Testament without disputing their accuracy. For instance, Jesus refers to creation (Mark 13:19), Noah and the flood (Matthew 24:37–39), and Jonah and the great fish (Matthew 12:38–41). In what ways does Jesus' mention of these events strengthen the claim that the events took place? In what ways could they still be disputed?

Some Well-Known Miracles of Jesus[9]	
MIRACLE	**SCRIPTURE PASSAGE**
Turns water into wine	John 2:1–11
Orders the wind and waves to be quiet	Mark 4:35–41
Walks on water	Matthew 14:22–33
With five loaves and two fishes, feeds a crowd of about 5,000 people	Matthew 14:13–21
Raises Lazarus to life	John 11:17–44
Raises a dead girl to life	Matthew 9:18–26
Gives sight to a man born blind	John 9:1–41
Cures the woman who had been bleeding for twelve years	Matthew 9:20–22

Some Well-Known Miracles of Jesus[9]	
Cures a man of evil spirits	Mark 5:1–20
Heals ten men with leprosy	Luke 17:11–19
Heals a crippled man	Mark 2:1–12
Heals a man who was deaf and could hardly talk	Mark 7:31–37
Heals the high priest's servant after the man's ear is cut off	Luke 22:49–52

12. Why do you think so many people today automatically deny that Jesus performed miracles?

What Now?

13. What personal struggles have you dealt with in the past or do you continue to face in accepting the supernatural portions of the Bible?

14. What information would you need to help you accept that some of these events really took place?

15. How could you present the evidence for supernatural parts of the Bible to a friend who is skeptical of the Bible's accuracy?

Consider This

On a scale of one to five, what response best describes your personal beliefs regarding the following miraculous portions of the Bible?

16. Noah's Ark and the flood that destroyed the earth's population:

1	2	3	4	5
Don't believe	Believe somewhat	Some of it is true	Mostly true	Completely accurate

17. Moses parting the Red Sea:

1	2	3	4	5
Don't believe	Believe somewhat	Some of it is true	Mostly true	Completely accurate

18. Jesus walking on the surface of the waters:

1	2	3	4	5
Don't believe	Believe somewhat	Some of it is true	Mostly true	Completely accurate

19. Jesus' resurrection from the dead on the third day:

1	2	3	4	5
Don't believe	Believe somewhat	Some of it is true	Mostly true	Completely accurate

20. What evidence do you still desire to find regarding the above miracles?

21. What are some of the other parts of the Bible that you struggle to accept as historically accurate?

SESSION 3

What about Those 'Lost Books' of the Bible?

Getting Started

In 2003, *The Da Vinci Code* sparked a renewed interest in what many call missing gospels or lost books of the Bible. Sir Teabing, the professor character in the novel, claimed that "More than eighty gospels were considered for the New Testament, and yet only a relative few were chosen for inclusion—Matthew, Mark, Luke and John." If that's true, even a little bit, isn't our current New Testament missing something missing? It would be true if the original followers of Jesus—James, Paul, and John—wrote eighty books during that same period that the early church had mentioned. But if books were written one or two hundred years later by writers with no connection to the disciples, should these be accepted as additional gospels? Of course the message of *The Da Vinci Code* suggests that these so-called "gospels" should be accepted.

Three years later, in 2006, *The Gospel of Judas* came to the public's attention. The document, dated as early as the middle of the second century, portrays a distinctly different version of Judas Iscariot than the New Testament's description of him as a traitor to Jesus. In contrast, this account claims that Judas had been secretly instructed to set Jesus up for crucifixion rather than serving as the bad guy. Is this true? If it is, what does that mean for the Gospels of the New Testament?

Today's bookstores and television specials continue to highlight these newly discovered books featuring intriguing alternative theories regarding early Christianity. They are promoting *The Gospel of Thomas*, *The Gospel of Mary Magdalene*, and *The Gnostic Bible*. What is the truth about these early writings? Did we only get our version of church history from the side that had the power? Is everything we have been told about Jesus and Christianity really wrong?

Once only the talk of spiritual-thriller novels, alternative theories regarding the foundations of the Christian faith now abound among the bestselling religious books of our time. In *The Jesus Papers*, we read about the bloodline of Jesus and Mary Magdalene. *The Jesus Dynasty* argues that the father of Jesus was really a Roman soldier from a neighboring town. In *The Jesus Family Tomb*, modern archaeologists claim to have found the actual tomb of Jesus, his wife, and child, complete with the bone boxes that contain DNA evidence of their relationships. Are all of these scholars completely wrong? Certainly they're at least partially right, aren't they?

Isn't it reasonable to think that there is more to the Bible than we know? There were no video cameras in the time of Jesus to record what He said or to capture the miracles He performed. Even if someone did take notes of His messages, how accurate could their notes be two thousand years later? Wouldn't something be lost in the details or the translation? There were no copy machine duplicates of Jesus' notes or transcripts of His messages.

Of course, this doesn't mean the books of the Bible are all wrong. If the writers of the New Testament books, for example, spent time with Jesus, then some of what they wrote must be accurate. But how do we know which parts are true and which parts are not? Maybe some of these missing gospels have just as much accurate information as Matthew, Mark, Luke, and John did.

For those who believe the Bible has been communicated in an accurate manner, these are important questions to explore. In this session, we will discuss the so-called lost gospels using a two-part approach. First, we'll feature some of the reasons the historical New Testament books can be trusted as an accurate historical account of events. Second, we'll highlight some of the reasons why these newly discovered gospel documents lack such historical support.

Talk about It

1. How can we tell what writings from history should be accepted as gospels and which ones should not? For instance, the biblical gospels were written during the lifetimes of the apostles. How is this different from other books sometimes labeled gospels today?

2. Why do you think that alternative theories about early Christianity and the books of the New Testament are so popular in our culture?

3. How does the fact that the Bible has been copied and translated numerous times throughout history influence your confidence in it?

Here's What I'm Thinking

How Did We Get the New Testament?

How did the teachings of Jesus and the apostles end up in our English translations of the twenty-first century? Five steps occurred in the process:

- First, Jesus taught his apostles until approximately AD 30.
- Second, His apostles publicly taught his message just 50 days after Jesus' death at the Pentecost holiday in Jerusalem.
- Third, people from several nations who had gathered in Jerusalem during Pentecost accepted this message, were baptized, and then returned to spread Christianity throughout the Roman Empire.
- Fourth, the apostles continued to lead the early church, correcting errors in teaching until AD 65–95.
- Fifth, the writings of the apostles began to circulate between AD 40–96 and were accepted by the early churches.

Therefore, no contradictions or differences in teaching existed during this time period. The New Testament documents began being copied and were later officially listed as the twenty-seven books we now have in our Bibles.

The Manuscripts of the New Testament Books

Sometimes people do not realize the enormous number of copies that exist of the New Testament manuscripts in comparison with other ancient documents. For example, few would dispute that Homer wrote the *Illiad* and that we have accurate copies of its contents. It is one of the best attested manuscripts of ancient history. Six hundred and forty-three copies of early manuscripts are known to be in existence, and the oldest copies we have were copied 500 years after Homer wrote the original manuscript.

When compared to most ancient works, that's a lot of copies for an ancient work, and a reasonable number of years between the original and the earliest transcribed copies known to be in existence. But can you believe that over 24,970 early remaining copies of portions of the New Testament exist? In some cases, less than fifty years separate the original New Testament manuscript and the earliest transcribed manuscript known to us today!

Historians use the following criteria when determining authenticity: 1) Are any original documents in our hands, or only copies? 2) If only copies exist, how old are they when compared with the approximate date of the original document? (The closer the copies are to the original, the better the chances of higher accuracy.) 3) How many copies exist? If there are only two or three, the evidence for authenticity is not as strong, especially when you compare those two or three copies to the 24,970 early manuscript portions of the New Testament.

Author[10]	Date Written	Earliest Copy	Approximate Time between original & copy	Number of Copies
Lucretius	died 55 or 53 BC	?	1100 yrs	2
Pliny	61–113 AD	850 AD	750 yrs	7
Plato	427–347 BC	900 AD	1200 yrs	7
Demosthenes	4th Cent. BC	1100 AD	1400 yrs	8
Herodotus	480–425 BC	900 AD	1300 yrs	8
Suetonius	75–160 AD	950 AD	800 yrs	8
Thucydides	460–400 BC	900 AD	1300 yrs	8
Euripides	480–406 BC	1100 AD	1500 yrs	9
Aristophanes	450–385 BC	900 AD	1200	10
Caesar	100–44 BC	900 AD	1000	10
Tacitus	circa 100 AD	1100 AD	1000 yrs	20
Aristotle	384–322 BC	1100 AD	1400	49
Sophocles	496–406 BC	1000 AD	1400 yrs	193
Homer (Iliad)	900 BC	400 BC	500 yrs	643
New Testament	50–100 AD	c. 130 AD and following	less than 100 years	24,970

4. How many of the classics listed above have no known originals in existence? How many years separate the original document and the earliest

known copy in some of the closest examples in the chart above?

5. Even if the copies of the Bible we have today are based on ancient manuscripts, do you think it's a problem that no original copies exist? Why or why not?

The Early Church Fathers

The church fathers were second and third generation converts of the apostles who personally served with Jesus. In addition to spreading the teachings as taught directly from the apostles, they helped affirm the acceptance and accuracy of the New Testament text from frequent references in their writings. For instance, Irenaeus quoted twenty-three of the twenty-seven New Testament books less than one hundred years after they were written, meaning he had access to this many books together within a generation of the apostles. This would have been a tremendous accomplishment for a culture whose writings could only be spread through handwritten copies. It has been mentioned by church historians that even if all 24,970 New Testament manuscripts disappeared, we could still reconstruct all but eleven verses using the quotes found in the writings of the early church fathers. Why? Because the church fathers included over 36,000 New Testament quotes within the first 300 years of Christianity.

New Testament Quotes from Early Church Leaders[11]					
Author	**Dates**	**Gospels/ Acts**	**Letters**	**Revelation**	**Total**
Justin Martyr	100–165	278	49	3	330
Irenaeus	120–212	1232	522	65	1819
Clement of Alexandria	150–216	1061	1334	11	2406
Origen	185–253	9580	8177	165	17,992
Tertullian	155–220	4324	2729	205	7258
Hippolytus	170–236	776	414	188	1378
Eusebius	260–340	3469	1680	27	5176
TOTAL		**20,720**	**14,905**	**664**	**36,289**

For example, Origen (185–253) noted that, "…according to the saying of the apostle, 'In whom dwelt all the fullness of the Godhead bodily.'" This is quoted from the apostle Paul in Colossians 2:9, and it is one of nearly eighteen thousand quotes by Origen from the New Testament.[12]

6. How do the numerous quotes found in the writings of early Christian leaders influence your view of the New Testament's accuracy?

7. How would you explain the importance of the manuscript evidence for the New Testament to someone seeking information about the Bible's accuracy?

What about the So-Called Missing Gospels?

Most of the books referred to when scholars discuss missing gospels are portions of a collection of documents called the *Nag Hammadi* texts, discovered in Egypt in 1945. What do these long-lost documents contain? Upon investigation, we find that most of these texts consist of books written over a hundred years after the New Testament Gospels by a group of people known as Gnostics. One scholar observes, "The *Nag Hammadi* Texts . . . are named after the place they were found on the west bank of the Nile. A library was found containing forty-five texts written in the Coptic language."[13] Notice, these were written from the early second century to the fourth century AD by people who lived long after Jesus' death and resurrection. Examples of these texts include *The Gospel of Thomas, The Gospel of Philip, The Acts of Peter*, and others. These texts were Gnostic in character and were found in a library of Gnostic work.

Early hints of Gnosticism were a problem even to Christians in the first century church. Yet the claim that later Gnostic works such as the *Nag Hammadi* documents are secret gospels can hardly withstand serious research. The church had known of these documents for centuries. Iraneaus (AD 130–200) and Tertullian (AD 160–225) actually refuted and dismissed these texts in their letters. None of these texts were ever considered part of the inspired writings of the apostles.

8. How do you feel about early church leaders describing certain books as containing inaccurate teachings about Jesus and Christianity? Does this seem appropriate based on the documents involved? Why or why not?

What about the Eighty Lost Gospels?

What about the other eighty or more lost gospels cited in *The Da Vinci Code* and mentioned in various ways by many popular nonfiction religious authors? Is there any evidence that back up such claims? Dr. Craig Blomberg, New Testament professor at Denver Seminary, writes, "Add up everything that was ever called a gospel in the first half-millennium of Christianity (most of which are small compilations of esoteric sayings ascribed to Jesus and not narratives of any portion of his life) and you come up with about two dozen documents."[14]

So do these extra gospels provide better information about Jesus than those in our New Testament? The contrast between these documents and the New Testament manuscripts is significant, both in number of manuscript copies and in content. More importantly, the biblical gospels existed earlier, carry much greater manuscript evidence, and hold the backing of church leaders from even the earliest times.

9. Based on what you have seen or heard on TV or other media, why do you think many people are interested in these other so-called gospels even when their authenticity is hardly trustworthy?

Why Didn't Non-Christian Writers Mention Jesus? Guess What—They Did!

Few people know that there are numerous ancient non-Christian writers who mention Christianity in their writings. According to historian and philosopher Dr. Gary Habermas, there are forty-five ancient sources pertaining to the life of Christ outside of the New Testament, including:

- 19 creedal statements
- 4 archaeological sources (such as stones, graves, tablets)
- 17 non-Christian, secular writings
- 5 extra-biblical Christian sources (early church fathers)
- In addition, there are numerous other church fathers and secular writers who mention Jesus shortly after the time period researched for these 45 sources, including the Gnostic documents mentioned above.

"Through this evidence [just the 45 earliest sources] we can substantiate 129 facts concerning the life, person, teachings, death, and resurrection of Jesus, plus the disciples' early message."[15] —Gary Habermas

---

Two early examples include Tacitus and Suetonius. Tacitus, who has been called the greatest historian of ancient Rome,[16] an individual generally acknowledged among scholars for his moral integrity, wrote in about AD 100 that:

> Consequently, to get rid of the report, Nero fastened the guilt and inflicted the most exquisite tortures on a class hated for their abominations, called Christians by the populace. *Christus* [Christ], from whom the name had its origin, suffered the extreme penalty during the reign of Tiberius at the hands of one of our procurators, Pontius Pilate, and a most mischievous superstition [Christ's resurrection] thus checked for the moment, again broke out not only in Judea, the first source of the evil, but even in Rome,

> where all things hideous and shameful from every part of the world find their center and become popular.[17]

In this report, we unearth six specific historical facts that agree with the New Testament:

1. Christians were named for their founder, *Christus* (Christ).
2. Christ was put to death by the Roman procurator Pontius Pilate.
3. This happened during the reign of Emperor Tiberius (between AD 14–37).
4. Christ's death ended the "superstition" [the Resurrection] for a short time.
5. Christianity spread from Judea where the teaching had its origin.
6. His followers carried this message to Rome.

Suetonius was chief secretary of Emperor Hadrian of Rome and had access to imperial records. Writing about AD 115, he noted, "Because the Jews at Rome caused continuous disturbances *at the instigation of Chrestus* [Christ], he expelled them from the city" (emphasis added).[18] In another place, he spoke regarding Christians and stated, "After the great fire at Rome. . . . Punishments were also inflicted on *the Christians, a sect professing a new and mischievous religious belief*" (emphasis added).[19] His account reveals three specific references to Christianity, including: 1) That it was Jesus who caused the Jews to make an uproar in Rome due to His teaching, 2) Suetonious describes Christianity's beliefs as mischievous, similar to how Tacitus records the concept of the resurrection, and 3) Suetonius specifically used the term Christians, referring to them as those who followed the teachings of Christ.

10. What difference does it make to you that many ancient non-Christian authors mention details regarding facts found in the New Testament?

What Now?

11. Based on the information shared in this session, how does this evidence affect your view of the reliability of the Bible?

12. If someone refuses to discuss the evidence that is shared in this chapter, do you think any amount of factual information would persuade them?

13. What areas do you feel you still need more information to feel comfortable about the accuracy of the Bible?

Consider This

Read the following statements and circle the response that best describes your opinion:

14. The Bible is an historically accurate book…
    A. on some occasions.
    B. on most issues.
    C. in every detail.
    D. I'm not sure what I believe about it.

15. The manuscript evidence for the New Testament...
    A. provides me further evidence that its words are true.
    B. is somewhat helpful in better understanding the Bible.
    C. doesn't really help persuade me either way.

16. Other so-called gospels...
    A. should not be considered to be as authoritative as the Bible.
    B. shouldn't be a big deal either way.
    C. contain their own truth as important as the New Testament gospels.
    D. I'm not sure what I think about this issue.

17. The evidence for the New Testament...
    A. makes me want to study it more since it strengthens my faith in Jesus.
    B. doesn't help me much either way.
    C. does not prove it is a reliable document.
    D. OTHER: ______________________________

SESSION 4

What about All of the Contradictions?

Getting Started

It has been said that the greatest cause of atheism in our world today is the hypocrisy of those who claim to be Christians. They claim to follow what Jesus taught, yet their lives reveal hidden issues that conflict with their professed beliefs. Today's media exposes and fixates on such tragedies in a way that strikes a significant blow in the minds of many skeptics. How can Christians do such things? Maybe the Bible they follow isn't quite what they claim after all.

However, problems with the messengers, while tragic, do not necessarily discredit the message itself. If you were told falsely that today was Wednesday but in reality it was really Thursday, would the false statement make the fact that it was actually Thursday wrong? Of course not. Even when the truth is distorted, the truth is still waiting to be discovered.

The only way we can discover what is true is through evaluating the *evidence*. For example, we can prove a man is lying if the man says he was in one location at a particular time when we have a video documenting that he was in a different location. This is routinely used in a court of law as evidence. If a woman tells you she is twenty-five years old when her driver's license says she is only nineteen, one of the two ages is wrong (or both). Both options cannot be accurate at the same time.

There are some cases when direct evidence like this is not available. In these situations, the information that is available can be used to determine the most likely scenario. Often in such situations, the integrity of the individuals involved is also used as an important factor in determining what really happened. For instance, parents would not likely entrust their children to a person they had never met before unless that person had a reputation that fit the requirements. If the individual has been a teacher for twenty years, has a list of references who can speak well on his or her behalf, and has passed a background check, then the person would be considered fairly trustworthy, even in a case when the person was previously unknown. Such a scenario takes place every day when managers seek to determine what employees to hire for available positions. No one can know all the details of a person's background. Instead, procedures are put into place to help locate the best person for a particular job.

In the case of the Bible, there is much more at stake than a job position. Our eternal destiny is on the line if the Bible is accurate. To accept its claims without reasonable investigation, however, is unnecessary. Any interested person can seek information about the Bible from outside sources, such as history, archaeology, science, and linguistics, to determine if the source is credible or not. If the Bible passes the test, then we can reasonably accept its teachings as true. If there are serious errors or contradictions, then it would be difficult to accept that it is a book from God and perfect.

Such contradictions would prove that the Bible is not the information God intended, but the words of humans who can and do report inaccuracies. If the Bible is inaccurate, then why accept it as coming from God? But if it is found to be accurate and without contradiction, then maybe it is exactly what it claims to be—the eternal, inspired word of God.

Talk about It

1. Have you ever discovered a secret about a person that disturbed or hurt you? What did it feel like to be misled?

2. People sometimes complain about contradictions in the Bible, but fail to mention specifics. What are some of the specific alleged contradictions people often use against the Bible?

3. Two major contradictions used against the Bible are: 1) How could a loving God allow evil in His world?, and 2) Why does the God of the Old Testament seem so much more judgmental than the God of the New Testament? Do you think these issues are contradictions? Why or why not?

4. If someone pointed out what they considered a contradiction in the Bible, how would you respond?

Here's What I'm Thinking

What Does It Mean to Say the Bible Is Inerrant or Inspired?

When scholars or pastors talk about the Bible being inspired, what do they mean? Volumes have been written on the topic, but the following three "I"s quickly communicate three of the main concepts used by scholars regarding the Bible:

Inspiration	God directed the human authors of the Bible to write down the words He desired, and they wrote them without error.
Inerrancy	The Bible is without error in all that it communicates.
Illumination	God's Spirit brings individual insight to those studying the Bible.

Contradictions between the God Portrayed in the Old and New Testament?

Many people think the God of the Old Testament is significantly different from the God of the New Testament. This is so troubling to some that they refuse to trust the Bible at all. Are there two different Gods? Did God change His ways?[20]

The Old Testament says that God...

- kicked Adam and Eve out of the Garden of Eden (see Genesis 3:16–23).
- killed everyone on earth except Noah's family during a worldwide flood (see Genesis 6–8).
- destroyed Sodom and Gomorrah, including innocent children (see Genesis 19).
- killed two of Aaron's sons because they were disobedient with their priestly work (see Leviticus 10:1–2).

- ordered the destruction of all people and animals in the city of Jericho except for the prostitute, Rahab and her family (see Joshua 6:21).

But the New Testament says that Jesus taught…

- "Do not resist an evil person" (Matthew 5:39).
- "Love one another. As I have loved you, so you must love one another" (John 13:34).
- "If you hold anything against anyone, forgive him" (Mark 11:25).

How can these two versions of God be reconciled? To start, let's look at God's nature: **1**) He is perfectly holy (Leviticus 11:45; Revelation 4:8); **2**) He is perfectly just (Deuteronomy 32:4; 2 Thessalonians 1:6); and **3**) He is perfectly loving (Deuteronomy 7:9; 1 John 4:16). This fundamental information about God is found in both the Old and New Testament.

Check out some of the verses below for yourself. God in the Old Testament is also revealed as loving, while God in the New Testament is also revealed as wrathful.

Further, the Old Testament *also* says that God is. . .

- "the compassionate and gracious God, slow to anger, abounding in love" (Exodus 34:6).
- "the faithful God, keeping his covenant of love" (Deuteronomy 7:9).
- "abounding in love and faithfulness" (Psalm 86:15).

And the New Testament says that Jesus *also* taught. . .

- "Whoever believes in the Son has eternal life, but whoever rejects the Son will not see life, for God's wrath remains on him" (John 3:36).

- "The wrath of God is being revealed from heaven against all the godlessness and wickedness of men who suppress the truth by their wickedness" (Romans 1:18).
- "The angels will come and separate the wicked from the righteous and throw them into the fiery furnace, where there will be weeping and gnashing of teeth" (Matthew 13:49–50).

A thorough examination of the evidence reveals a God whose nature is consistently loving and just.

5. In what ways might your view of God need to be revised based on the information presented above?

6. How does such an examination of the character of God help strengthen your view of the Bible's accuracy?

Handling Alleged Bible Contradictions

This is one of the more common allegations about the Bible, but it is certainly not the only example. How can we approach apparent conflicts in Scripture? The following steps can be used to help determine the specifics of allegations you face yourself or in conversations with others:

- ***Define the issue***: What *exactly* do you (or the other person) see as the alleged contradiction?

  Example: Who carried the cross of Jesus? Matthew, Mark, and Luke report that Simon from Cyrene was told by a Roman soldier to carry the cross for Him. But John *seems to suggest* that Jesus carried it the whole way himself: "Carrying his own cross, he went out to the place of the Skull (which in Aramaic is called Golgotha)" (John 19:17).

- ***Determine the options***: What are the *potential options* that could explain this situation?

  Example: In this case, either: **1**) Jesus carried His cross the entire trip, **2**) Simon carried the cross the entire trip, or **3**) Jesus carried it part of the way and Simon carried it after Jesus fell with the cross. (Of course, some would suggest the account is non-historical, inaccurate, unverifiable, or that none of the answers is correct. However, our goal here is to determine whether the Bible is stating a contradiction or not.)

- ***Develop each option's strengths and weaknesses***: Which option or options make the most sense?

  Example: **Choice 1** above would imply that Simon didn't carry the cross at all and that there is an apparent contradiction between the gospel accounts. However, it is possible Simon indeed carried the cross, since John mentions this. Therefore, both possibilities could be correct if Jesus began carrying the cross, fell down under its weight along the way to Golgotha, and then the Roman soldier commanded Simon to carry it the rest of the way.

- ***Decide on a most likely scenario***: Where does all of the evidence lead?

  Example: **Choice 3, suggesting** that Jesus carried His cross, fell under its weight, and then Simon carried it the rest of the way, seems the most likely scenario. In this case, there is no reason to suggest a contradiction, and this scenario accounts for all of the evidence. To be a contradiction, John would have had to say, "Jesus carried His cross all the way to the place of the Skull." But John didn't say this. The claim that this is a contradiction does not stand up under close scrutiny of the verses involved.

7. Does the type of research shared above help you in handling Bible difficulties? Why or why not?

8. How could these guidelines help you in discussing apparent Bible contradictions with others?

Contradictions in the Resurrection Accounts?

When the four Gospels present the details of Jesus' death, burial, and resurrection, a quick reading of the texts has led some people to assume that the accounts contradict each other; therefore, they assume the resurrection itself is questionable or cannot be trusted. So we must ask, do the four resurrection narratives of the Gospels of Matthew, Mark, Luke, and John in any way contradict each other?

We must start by remembering that the gospel writers are independently reporting these events. A hallmark of independent reporting is differences in content. In a court of law, for example, it is *often true* that four witnesses describing a traffic accident (or a crime, or any other incident) will each supply different details. Each witness notices and reports those things that are unique, relevant, or important to that person. The same is true for the gospel writers. Each one devotes differing amounts of space and detail to the events. Each mentions some details that the others do not.

If every gospel writer recorded the events in precisely the same way, giving precisely the same details, this would be evidence of writing together rather than using independent testimony. There is no reason to demand that the gospel writers report the same details. When critics charge that contradictions exist merely because the accounts differ, they are being unfair. They are holding the gospel authors to a standard to which they would not subject themselves.

For example, when the *Challenger* Space Shuttle exploded or the Twin Towers went down on 9/11, many of us probably flipped from channel to channel to catch different news accounts of the events. Different facts were added or omitted by different reporters. But such differences didn't lead us to conclude that the incidents never happened.

Furthermore, if one of the channels added new information or gave a slightly different emphasis in their report, did we assume that the various news accounts could not be harmonized? Not at all. The same is true for the Gospels. When one writer gives additional information or places his own emphasis on one part of the story, no contradiction need be assumed.

Here is just one example: Do the four resurrection narratives contradict each other concerning the number of women who went to Jesus' tomb?

- Matthew mentions *two* women—Mary Magdalene and the other Mary (28:1).
- Mark mentions *three* women—Mary Magdalene, Mary the mother of James, and Salome (16:1).
- Luke *does not specify a number* but simply mentions "the women" (24:1).
- John mentions *one* woman, Mary Magdalene (20:1).

Mark feels it is important, for some reason, to report that Salome was at the tomb, while Matthew does not. Perhaps Salome was the woman, or one of several women, who recounted the events to Mark. Perhaps Matthew does not mention Salome because he documented the event from a source that did not mention her.

Some critics charge that Luke disagrees with Matthew and Mark because he mentions only "the women." But none of the gospel writers say it was *only* two women, or *only* one woman, or *only* three women. Each writer mentions those he wants to recognize, *but none of them give contradictory information.* If one of the four writers had said *only* so-and-so went to the tomb, and another said *only* somebody else went, then we would have a contradiction.

In referring to "the women," Luke does not contradict Matthew and Mark; he is merely less specific. Similarly, John does not contradict the other three writers because he mentions only one woman, Mary Magdalene, going to the tomb. Two perfectly reasonable explanations present themselves here.

First, all the women may have set out for the tomb, with Mary arriving first. John simply records the earliest arrival. Or second, John may have chosen to write only about Mary, even though he could have written about all of them. These possibilities are, of course, not mutually exclusive.

As with the other writers, John does not say that *only* Mary Magdalene went to the tomb. But he is perfectly free to concentrate on Mary Magdalene, especially if her experience is important to his writing interests. He probably featured her for a number of reasons: **1**) After the resurrection, Jesus appeared to her first (and not to one of the disciples); **2**) Mary looked into the tomb and saw the two angels (John 20:11–12); **3**) Mary personally met the resurrected Jesus near the empty tomb (verses 11–18); and **4**) Jesus commissioned her to go and tell the disciples the good news (verse 17).

The disciples who heard the women tell their stories may have heard bits from each of the women, most of it from just one, or most of it from several.

In *The Easter Enigma,* John Wenham suggests that "Luke's is a straightforward account written from Joanna's point of view (see Luke 8:3; 24:10), whereas Mark's is an account written from the point of view of the other three women."[21] Similarly, John, at a later date when the other three Gospels were already well known, may have written his version strictly from Mary Magdalene's viewpoint, assuming that the majority of Christians already knew that this group of women had gone to the tomb. Perhaps he decided to share additional details of what had happened to Mary Magdalene because they were less familiar to his readers.

Indeed, when Luke mentions "the others with them" (24:10), we could even assume that more than three women were present at the tomb on that first Easter morning. If Luke is describing the women who actually visited the tomb, then there were at least five women—Joanna and "the others" indicate at least one more person than Salome. It is also possible that the "other women" to whom Luke alludes were part of the group who reported to the disciples.

To sum up, we know that at least three women visited the tomb, and possibly more. The resurrection accounts are not contradictory. None of the writers state that only a set number of women visited the tomb. Critics read that into the scenario. Rather, each writer selected details from a broader pool of evidence according to his purpose in writing.

9. Do you think that investing time and energy to answer apparent Bible contradictions for yourself and others is important? Why or why not?

What Now?

10. In what ways can answering Bible difficulties for others help them to believe that the Bible is an accurate book?

11. If the Bible is really God's Word, why do you think He hasn't removed the portions that appear to some people as contradictions?

12. Why do people sometimes intentionally try to find problems or contradictions in the Bible? What might this approach say about the person's attitude toward seeking truth?

Consider This

Select the choice that best represents your opinion right now regarding the following statements:

13. Apparent Bible contradictions show me that...
    A. The Bible clearly contains contradictions.
    B. The Bible might have some contradictions, but I need to investigate further.
    C. I should believe the Bible is God's Word because there are reasonable answers for all alleged contradictions.

14. When I encounter possible contradictions in the Bible, I prefer to...
    A. Study to determine the most likely truth of the issue.
    B. Reject the parts I do not understand.
    C. See if I can work through the alleged conflicts because the Bible is a trustworthy book.
    D. Ignore the apparent contradictions because they're not that big of a deal.

SESSION 5

Why Do Christians Believe the Bible Is Perfect?

Getting Started

Why do many Christians believe the Bible is a perfect, God-inspired book without error? Have these people really read what's inside of it? In the first book, God tells Abraham to burn his son as a sacrifice. Even though God later told him to stop, what kind of God would do such a thing?

The next book, Exodus, tells us God killed Pharaoh's firstborn son along with the firstborn son of every family in the area, except for those of the Israelites, because Pharaoh refused to let the Israelites go. The book later includes various food laws, rules about skin infections, and guidelines for sacrificing animals. How could such content become the most printed book in the history of the world?

Endless lists of genealogies, travel journals of one nation for forty years in the desert, people who lived nine hundred years, a shepherd boy killing a soldier that was over nine feet tall—is this the book Christians believe is inspired by God?

The science also appears a little out of date. The universe created in six days, the sun standing still for Joshua, the Red Sea parting for Moses, Jesus causing a fig tree to wither on demand? Yet these words continue to be read in churches all around the world every Sunday and every day throughout the week among countless devoted followers.

Maybe we could accurately say that the Bible is an extremely popular book that is highly valued among numerous people. But it is another thing altogether to claim that because it is very popular, this book comes from God and should be considered divinely inspired. How can anyone defend the claim that we should accept the words of the Bible as not only historically accurate, but as having a divine status as inspired writing—the inspired Word of God?

"There is no body of ancient literature in the world which enjoys such a wealth of good textual attestation as the New Testament."[22] —F.F. Bruce

---

Sure, you can say cities cited in the Bible have been found in the Middle East. So what? Does that mean we should believe Jonah was really swallowed by a big fish and was spit out three days later? You can argue all day long that there are thousands of manuscript copies of the Bible that accurately transmit the words of the originals, but does that make the originals the inspired Word of God? Not necessarily.

Why does one book written in the Middle East thousands of years ago get to tell us how to live our lives today? Did those shepherds and fishermen know the struggles people would have today? How do we know for sure they heard from God when they wrote the book?

What it really comes down to is whether the Bible contains some truth or whether it is all the truth of God. Many people would agree that it includes some positive morals and wise teachings. It is full of ancient wisdom that can be applied in certain ways today. But what can be said that would make a person believe that the Bible is more than just another holy book, more than one of many sacred writings? What can be said to suggest that the Bible is more than just good, but that it is inspired and without error?

Talk about It

1. What information would someone need to provide in order to prove that any writings (such as the Qu'ran, Book of Mormon, or *I Ching*) are not just special words, but God's words?

2. Has there been a time in your life when you have attempted to figure out if a particular book (the Bible or another book) was really from God? If so, where did your search lead? If not, what would it take to make you want to begin such an intense personal study?

Here's What I'm Thinking

What the Bible Says Is What God Says (and Vice Versa)

A quick reading of almost any part of the Bible shows that it uses statements regarding what God said and what Scripture says on a regular basis. For example, Exodus 9:6 states:

> And the next day *the LORD did it*: All the livestock of the Egyptians died, but not one animal belonging to the Israelites died. (emphasis added)

Here, we have a written account of something God had promised would happen to the Egyptians if they did not obey His warning. Notice what this same account is called in Romans 9:17:

> For *the Scripture says* to Pharaoh: "I raised you up for this very purpose, that I might display my power in you and that my name might be proclaimed in all the earth." (emphasis added)

The apostle Paul equated these words from Exodus with "Scripture." He considered these words the very words of God.

The following chart highlights many examples that show these connections:

God said	=	**Scripture says**
Genesis 12:3		Galatians 3:8
Exodus 9:6		Romans 9:17

Bible said	=	**God said**
Genesis 2:24		Matthew 19:4–5
Psalms 95:7		Hebrews 3:7
Psalms 2:1		Acts 4:24–25
Isaiah 55:3		Acts 13:34
Psalms 16:10		Acts 13:35
Psalms 2:7		Hebrews 1:5
Psalms 97:7		Hebrews 1:6
Psalms 104:4		Hebrews 1:7

Some would suggest this is circular reasoning, since the Bible is used to prove that the Bible is inspired, but that is missing the point. The Bible must refer to itself as Scripture if the information actually is the Word of God. We can be sure it makes that claim. After we understand clearly that it claims to be Scripture, the Word of God, we can examine the evidence for this claim. The point is that the two are so integrated in the Bible that if the Bible is true, then it must be the inspired words of God.

3. How does the fact that the Bible says what God says influence your view of the Bible as God's Word? Is it helpful to you? Why or why not?

If Jesus Was God, What Did He Say about the Bible?

Jesus Christ is the One who claimed to be God and proved His claim by rising from the dead. It is on His authority as God of the universe that we are sure the Bible is the Word of God. Jesus confirmed the Old Testament's authority, as well as an authoritative New Testament through His disciples. Jesus affirmed the Old Testament to be the Word of God and promised to guide His disciples to know all truth. Jesus claimed for the Bible:

- Divine authority (Matthew 4:4, 7, 10)
- Indestructibility (Matthew 5:17–18)
- Infallibility (John 10:35)
- Ultimate supremacy (Matthew 15:3, 6)
- Factual inerrancy (Matthew 22:29; John 17:17)
- Historical reliability (Matthew 12:40, 24:37–38)
- Scientific accuracy (Matthew 19:4–5; John 3:12)[23]

If Jesus is God's Son, then His perfect life, His predictions of the future, His resurrection from the dead, and all of His authority affirm that the Bible is the Word of God. According to Dr. Norman Geisler:

> Jesus taught definitely that God was the originator of the Hebrew Old Testament.

> He taught as authoritative or authentic most of the books of the Hebrew canon. . . . he asserted that the Old Testament as a whole was unbreakable Scripture (John 10:35); that it would never perish (Matthew 5:18); and that it must be fulfilled (Luke 24:44). . . . Jesus not only defined the limits . . . but he laid down principles of canonicity.[24]

In other words, *if Jesus is who He says He is then the Bible is what He says it is.*

We also must understand that we do not *begin* by arguing that the Bible is inspired and therefore automatically true when it speaks about Jesus. That would be a circular argument. Rather, we begin with the question, "Do we have accurate information in the four Gospels about Jesus?" We begin with historical *accuracy.*

This would be true of any book. We believe the phone book is accurate, but we don't think it's inspired. We read biographies of famous individuals in history in order to understand what happened during their time, and we generally accept these accounts as accurate. With the Bible, we first realize that Jesus claimed to be God, was crucified, buried, and that the tomb was soon empty. The big question then becomes, "Does the evidence show that Jesus came back to life from the dead?" If so, then He is God. Only then do we ask, "If Jesus is God, then what did He teach about the Bible?" If He taught that it was the inspired Word of God, we believe it on the basis of His *authority.* In this way, our argument is not circular, but based upon all of the evidence.

4. In what ways are the issues of the Bible's inspiration and the person of Jesus intertwined?

5. If God says the Bible is perfect and Jesus says the Bible is perfect, then what must we conclude about the Bible's contents?

What Does It Mean to Say the Bible Is Inerrant?

To say something is inerrant is to claim that something is without error. Applied to the Bible, inerrancy means that its original text is completely accurate, true, and perfect in every way. However, inerrancy has become a highly technical term within theology, so it important to explain exactly what inerrancy does and does not claim.

What inerrancy *does* claim:

1. Inerrancy means that what the Bible teaches is true without a single error in the original manuscripts. Dr. Paul Feinberg defines inerrancy as follows: "Inerrancy means that when all facts are known, the Scriptures in their original autographs and properly interpreted will be shown to be wholly true in everything that they affirm, whether that has to do with doctrine or morality or with the social, physical, or life sciences.[25]

   A more concise definition would be, "What Scripture says, God says—through human agents and without error."[26]

2. To apply equally to all parts of Scripture, inerrancy must apply equally to all parts of Scripture as it was originally written. It would be inconsistent to believe in limited inerrancy (some parts are true and others aren't). This would require that a fallible interpreter become an infallible discerner and interpreter of the "Word of God" within the Scriptures. This

only opens the door for confusion and uncertainty in interpretation based upon either subjectivism or personal bias.

3. Those with a skeptical viewpoint of the Bible sometimes first assume errors in the Bible and then have little trouble finding them (from their perspective). However, the proper way to interpret the Bible involves a respect for the text as given until proven otherwise. In other words, due attention is given to the claim that first and foremost the Bible is truly telling us information God wants us to know. Also, interpretation must involve an objective and impartial methodology. If one does not first determine the authority of Scripture and second, discover what the original author was conveying at the time he wrote the text, a person is really incapable of saying whether or not the information is true or false.

What inerrancy does *not* claim:

1. Christians commonly hold to the doctrine of biblical inerrancy on the authority of Jesus, realizing that it does not guarantee that we will be able to authoritatively give the final solution to every alleged problem passage. Given the present limited state of human knowledge, no one can logically expect proof when the means of proof are absent. For example, we are still learning the exact meanings of some words used in the Old and New Testaments. We do not yet know every custom from every period in biblical history. Proof of inerrancy is therefore limited by our present state of knowledge. Nevertheless, such realities in no way deny or disprove inerrancy, especially when the weight of the evidence so

strongly supports inerrancy. It is very impressive to realize many opportunities have existed within the biblical record to disprove inerrancy, yet it remains capable of rational defense after nearly two thousand years. Again, the fact that historically, alleged errors are routinely proven later to be truths when more knowledge becomes available is equally impressive. (For further information on researching Bible difficulties, we recommend Dr. Gleason Archer's *Handbook of Bible Difficulties*.)

2. Inerrancy does not refer to thousands of manuscript copies or translations, but only to the original manuscripts. Copies and translations may be considered inerrant only to the degree they reproduce the originals.

3. Inerrancy does not claim absolute precision. Approximations in numbers, for example, are not errors. To illustrate, no one would argue it was an error to say the following:

- I earned $40,000 last year (it was really $40,200).
- In 1995 I received my college degree (it was June of 1995).
- What a lovely sunset (the earth's rotation appears as the sun setting).
- Look! There just ain't no free lunch! (breaking the rules of grammar to emphasize a point).
- Steve went to the store (he also stopped by the pool on the way back).

In the interest of improved communication we often use approximations or statements that are technically incorrect in grammar, number, science, history, etc. This is also true of the biblical writers: their purpose was to communicate, not to write in technicalities. Inerrancy does not demand that every word in the Bible be written in technical language or with knowledge of modern twenty-first century science, which would certainly make it a book closed to all but the specialist. Also, precision may become overly precise and thus awkward or useless during communication. To speak of a setting sun is not error in spite of its scientific imprecision.[27]

6. Does the idea of the Bible being an inspired and inerrant book from God appeal to you or not? Why would it be important for you to know if a book was the inspired Word of God that we could read for our lives today?

7. In what ways is the idea of the Bible as God's inspired and inerrant Word based on factual evidence? In what ways does it seem to be based on faith?

Explaining Fulfilled Prophecy

Many use the fact of fulfilled prophecy as a strong indication that the Bible is God's Word. For example, when originally written, over one-fourth of the Bible was predictive in nature:

Surprising Facts Concerning Bible Prophecy

- Approximately 27% of the entire Bible contains prophetic material. Half of that has already come true. Half remains to be fulfilled.
- Of the Old Testament's 23,210 verses, 6,641 contain prophetic material, or 28.5%.

- Of the New Testament's 7,914 verses, 1,711 contain prophetic material, or 21.5%.
- Of the Bible's 31,124 verses, 8,352 contain prophetic material, or 27% of the whole Bible.
- 1,800 verses deal with the Second Coming of Christ.
- In the New Testament, 318 verses deal with the Second Coming of Christ.
- Approximately one out of every 25 Bible verses in the New Testament refers to the Second Coming.[28]

Hundreds of biblical prophecies have been fulfilled with precise detail. Not once has a prediction of the Bible been proven as wrong. Four hundred and fifty-six different prophecies have been identified from the Old Testament that directly predict aspects of the life of Jesus Christ. Here are two quick points to examine first. Daniel predicted the exact year the Messiah would appear (483 years later) on earth (Daniel 9:25). Second, here are twenty-four specific prophecies about Christ that were fulfilled in the last twenty-four hours of His life on Earth:

24 Prophecies Fulfilled in the 24 Hours before Jesus' Death

#	Prophecy	Prediction	Fulfillment
1	Betrayed by a friend	Psalm 55:12–14	Matthew 26:49–50
2	Money thrown to the potter	Zechariah 11:13	Matthew 27:5–7
3	Abandoned by His followers	Zechariah 13:7	Matthew 26:56
4	Accused by false witnesses	Psalm 35:11	Matthew 26:59–60
5	Beaten and spat upon	Isaiah 50:6	Matthew 27:30
6	Silent before His accusers	Isaiah 53:7	Matthew 27:12–14

24 Prophecies Fulfilled in the 24 Hours before Jesus' Death *(continued)*			
7	Wounded and bruised	Isaiah 53:5	Matthew 27:26, 29
8	Fell under the cross	Psalm 109:24	John 19:17
9	Hands and feet pierced	Psalm 22:16	Luke 23:33
10	Crucified with thieves	Isaiah 53:12	Mark 15:17–18
11	Prayed for those who killed Him	Isaiah 53:12	Luke 23:34
12	People shook their heads	Psalm 109:25	Matthew 27:39
13	People ridiculed Him	Psalm 22:8	Matthew 27:41–43
14	People astonished	Psalm 22:17	Luke 23:35
15	Clothes taken and cast lots	Psalm 22:18	John 19:23–24
16	Cries for the forsaken	Psalm 22:1	Matthew 27:46
17	Given gall and vinegar	Psalm 69:21	John 19:28–29
18	Committed Himself to God	Psalm 31:5	Luke 23:46
19	Friends stood at a distance	Psalm 38:11	Luke 23:49
20	Bones not broken	Psalm 34:20	John 19:33, 36
21	Heart broken	Psalm 22:14	John 19:34
22	Side pierced	Zechariah 12:10	John 19:34–37
23	Darkness over the land	Amos 8:9	Matthew 27:45
24	Buried in a rich man's tomb	Isaiah 53:9	Matthew 27:57–60

What are the chances of such predictions being made by random luck or guesswork? Mathematicians have estimated that the possibility of sixteen of these prophecies being fulfilled by chance is about 1 in 10 to the 45th power. That's a decimal point followed by 44 zeroes and a 1![29] These figures show it is impossible that these prophecies could have been fulfilled by accident. Before Jesus came to earth, many Jews read these prophecies regarding the Messiah and believed they were about a future person. Jesus' life showed that they were indeed about a future person, and that the future had now arrived in the form of this "carpenter's son" from Nazareth.

Scientists generally accept a standard that anything with a possibility of less than one chance in ten to the 50th power is regarded as impossible of happening by chance.

---

9. How does the fact of fulfilled Bible prophecy influence your opinion of the Bible's inspiration?

10. In what ways does fulfilled prophecy prove that the Bible is true?

What Now?

11. Do you believe it is enough to simply accept that the Bible is God's Word without investigating it for yourself? Why or why not?

12. Other than factual evidence, what other factors could contribute to you or someone else not accepting the Bible as God's inspired and inerrant Word?

13. How would a viewpoint that the Bible is really God's Word influence the way you studied and applied the Bible's teachings?

Consider This

14. Choose the following aspects about the Bible that you currently believe are true. (Check all that apply.)
    ___ The Bible is a generally accurate book.
    ___ The Bible is a book full of helpful teachings.
    ___ The Bible contains sayings from God.
    ___ The Bible is God's inspired and inerrant Word.

15. My interest in the Bible:
    ___ I want to learn more about the Bible.
    ___ I am willing to commit to further study of the Bible's teachings and their application for my life.
    ___ I believe the Bible is God's Word and desire to make it a major part of my life from this point forward.

16. My desire to tell others about the Bible:
    ___ I am unsure what I want to say about the Bible to others.
    ___ I want to tell others about what I am learning from the Bible, but I'm not sure how to do it.
    ___ I am committed to finding ways to tell others about the perfect teachings I have discovered in the Bible.

SESSION 6

How Do We Know the Words Haven't Been Changed?

Getting Started

Today's marketing can make any product seem to be the most exciting breakthrough ever discovered. How many ways can a commercial be produced to sell a bar of soap, a soft drink, or the latest toy? There is no end to the creativity of those wishing to promote the sales of a product when a company depends on its results for success.

Some suggest the same techniques have been used in the production and transmission (handwritten copying) of Bible manuscripts. The Bible claims to teach what God has said in past generations, along with how to know Jesus Christ personally as God's Son. But was it simply developed to appeal to a particular audience of people to "market" Jesus for success? How can we be certain that words and concepts have not been adapted to better target groups of people in the process of expanding Christianity?

Religious extremists have certainly succeeded in utilizing spiritual concepts in order to obtain and manipulate followers. Such groups usually operate in a seemingly innocent fashion, offering friendship and purpose—yet the leader is ultimately a fraud. Is it possible that Christianity falls in the same category as other non-Christian religious scams? How is it any different? How can we tell that the teachings of the Bible are any more accurate?

When we search the facts about the authors of the Bible's books, we must consider that personal bias could be involved. Maybe the original group of writers conspired together to promote Jesus. Perhaps those who later copied the documents manipulated the words of their texts to reflect their own personal preferences or to gain an advantage. What must be determined is whether Christianity's claims are true: that the Bible is more reliable than books or documents linked to any other religion—or any other book for that matter—especially when it speaks of supernatural miracles and issues of eternity.

In today's studies of the New Testament, for instance, it is alleged that the books of the New Testament were not arranged in their current form until the fourth century, three hundred years after the events. Even if the accounts did not contain legends by this time, they certainly could have been changed to adapt to new audiences as Christianity spread, couldn't they? Shouldn't our investigation of the Bible include discussion as to how the present form of the Scriptures came to us? If the words in the Bible really are God's words, then there should have been some type of process in place to make sure His words stayed intact and unaltered to impact us today.

In this discussion, we'll discuss three key issues surrounding this issue: **1**) the credibility of the original authors, **2**) the historical process of copying the books of the Bible and how they came down to us through the years, and **3**) the changed lives of those who follow the Bible's teachings today.

Talk about It

1. When was a time you copied down a message or note from someone and later discovered you had recorded the information inaccurately? What happened?

2. How does knowing that Jesus did not personally write any of the New Testament's books affect your opinion of the Bible? If you do consider the Bible a reliable source concerning the life of Jesus, on what do you base this reliability?

3. What accusations have you commonly heard about errors in the copies of the Bible? How have these accusations influenced how you view the Bible?

Here's What I'm Thinking

The Original Documents Fit the Facts

Sir Frederick Kenyon, former director and principle librarian of the British Museum, wrote about the whole process of when the books of the New Testament were written down, when they were copied, and how close the copies we have today are to the original documents. What did he discover? Sir Kenyon wrote:

> In no other case [in ancient history] is the interval of time between the composition of the book and the date of the earliest extant [existing] manuscripts so short as in that of the New Testament. The interval, then, between the dates of original composition and the earliest extant evidence [existing copies] become so small as to be in fact negligible, and the last foundation for any doubt that *the Scriptures have come down to us substantially as they were written*, has now been removed. Both the authenticity and the general integrity of the books of the New Testament may be regarded as finally established.[30] (emphasis added)

The gospel writers themselves either claim to be eyewitnesses or base their accounts on the direct spoken and written testimonies of eyewitnesses of Jesus' life. For example, Luke began his gospel with the words:

> Many have undertaken to draw up an account of the things that have been fulfilled among us, just as they were handed down to us by those who from the first were eyewitnesses and servants of the word. Therefore, since I myself have carefully investigated everything from the beginning, it seemed good also to me to write an orderly account for you, most excellent Theophilus, so that you may know the certainty of the things you have been taught. (Luke 1:1–4)

The short interval of time between the events related in the gospels and the writing of the gospels themselves also strengthens the claims that the accounts are based on eyewitness reports. The following chart illustrates the traditional dates of the four Gospels:

Gospel	Approximate date	Years from events
Matthew	AD 50–60s	20–30
Mark	50–60s (some date Mark as early as the mid-40s)	20–30
Luke	60	30
John	85–90	55–60

Notice that in each case, the books came out when the people who had witnessed Jesus' life, both friends and enemies, were still living. Both sides would have quickly pointed out any historical inaccuracies from the facts they had witnessed.

Further, the New Testament books were authored by a small group of individuals who were all in some way connected directly with Jesus. All of the New Testament books were connected in some way with the twelve apostles and the teachings of Jesus through the following nine sources:

- Two apostles, **Matthew** (1) and **John** (2), wrote gospels. John also wrote three letters and Revelation.
- **Peter** (3), an apostle, authored two letters and was the source for **Mark's** (4) gospel.
- **Luke** (5) based his gospel on the eyewitness testimony of the apostles. He was also a traveling companion of the apostle Paul. Paul later quotes Luke's gospel as Scripture in 1 Timothy 5:18.
- **James** (6) and **Jude** (7) were brothers of Jesus. James did not believe in Christ until after the resurrection

of Jesus. James later became bishop of the Jerusalem Church and wrote the New Testament book of James. Jude became a convert after the resurrection as well, writing the book that bears his name.

- **The author of Hebrews** (8) was well known to his recipients but not to everyone in the church. This delayed its acceptance to some. Many claim the author was Barnabas, a fellow missionary with Paul. (Many others believe that Paul himself wrote the epistle.)
- **Paul** (9), the missionary apostle, authored at least 13 of the 27 New Testament books and was recognized as writing authoritative Scripture by Peter.[31]

Nine individuals wrote the 27 books received by the churches and recognized as Scripture (eight if Paul wrote Hebrews). All but John's books were written and received by AD 75, with most books written within forty-five years of the events of Jesus' life. Within approximately one generation of the New Testament's completion, every book in the New Testament had been cited by a church father.[32]

4. How does the fact that the New Testament was written in the appropriate time period and by a select group of people associated with Jesus influence your view of the Bible's accuracy?

5. How does the early expansion and rapid growth of Christianity positively affect your view of the Bible's accuracy?

Why Are There So Many Variations in the Manuscripts?

When we compare the 24,970 ancient manuscript copies of the New Testament that have come down to us, we realize some copies leave a word out or put it in a different place in the sentence. Others add an extra phrase to a sentence. What can we say about these variants (differences) in the copies? How do we know the exact way the author wrote the sentence?

Some scholars have estimated that there are as many as 150,000 differences among the numerous early manuscripts of the New Testament.[33] How does anyone really believe we can figure out which copies are the original wording?

The answer lies in a correct understanding of *what kind* of differences exist. Suppose we have five manuscript copies of an original document that no longer exists. Each copy is different:

Manuscript #1: Jesus Christ is the Savior of the whole worl.
Manuscript #2: Christ Jesus is the Savior of the whole world.
Manuscript #3: Jesus Christ s the Savior of the whole world.
Manuscript #4: Jesus Christ is th Savior of the whle world.
Manuscript #5: Jesus Christ is the Savor of the whole wrld.

Could we figure out which version was closest to the original and therefore the most authoritative? Unless the apostles wrote in slang or with typos, then we would agree this is not an impossible challenge. Conservative scholars comment that over ninety-nine percent of such "variants" are of this nature and therefore easily corrected.[34]

In fact, the proximity to the original text and the multiplicity of the manuscripts enable textual scholars to accurately reconstruct the original text with more than ninety-nine percent accuracy. Renowned Greek scholar Sir Frederic Kenyon affirmed that all manuscripts agree on the essential correctness of ninety-nine percent of the verses in the New Testament. Another noted Greek scholar, A.T. Robertson, said the real concern of the controversies surrounding the original wording of the New Testament is on "a thousandth part of the entire text."[35] Furthermore, the one-tenth of a percent in dispute does not influence any foundational belief.

6. Does the accurate reconstruction of the New Testament's books strengthen your belief in the Bible as God's Word? Why or why not?

7. Why do you think there are variations in the manuscripts of the Bible? Do you consider the large number of ancient copies in existence a fact that helps prove the Bible's accuracy or disproves it due to the variations among manuscripts?

Why Do the Copies of the Bible's Manuscripts Contain Errors?

Today's technologies allow for the duplication of materials at a level of extreme accuracy. For instance, when copies of *The New York Times* are produced and distributed nationwide, each copy of a particular day's paper is exactly alike from a textual standpoint. Automated systems of computers and printers provide a miniscule level of error even on the scale of millions of copies.

Such was not the case centuries ago. There was not a local FedEx Kinko's® down the street to reproduce Paul's latest letter or the prophecies of Isaiah. Instead, every copy of every document required word-by-word, letter-by-letter hand copying. An entire industry of professional scribes existed during the first century (AD) that specifically wrote dictations and duplications of important works for those with the funds to pay for them.

Because of such a comparatively primitive system of transmission, some have argued that the Bible we have today cannot be trusted. After centuries of scribal inaccuracies, they argue that substantial changes must have taken place. One recent *New York Times* bestseller provocatively titled *Misquoting Jesus*, suggests:

> In some instances, the very meaning of the text is at stake, depending on how one resolves a textual problem: Was Jesus an angry man [Mark 1.41]? Was he completely distraught in the face of death [Heb 2.8–9]? Did he tell his disciples that they could drink poison without being harmed [Mark 16.9–20]? Did he let an adulteress off the hook with nothing but a mild warning [John 7.53–8.11]? Is the doctrine of the Trinity explicitly taught in the New Testament [1 John 5.7–8]? Is Jesus actually called "the unique God" there [John 1.18]? Does the New Testament indicate that even the Son of God himself does not know when the end will come [Matt 24.36]? The questions go on and on, and all of them are related to how one resolves difficulties in the manuscript tradition as it has come down to us.[36]

Concerning this quote and others you might see, remember this: It's one thing to make such claims against the writings concerning Jesus. It's quite another to defend your claims. Each of the above examples in Scripture has been addressed by language scholars, and their analysis should strengthen your confidence in the text. (For a full response, check out the articles in the "Bible" section at www.johnankerberg.org.)

When we talk about the accuracy of the New Testament's transmission, what we really want to know is if *what was written then is what we have now*. We don't really care that much if someone accidentally put an extra "T" on the end of a word or duplicated a letter. We're concerned whether the writings left by those who spent time with Jesus during the first century are still available for our study today.

So why are there errors among the ancient manuscripts? There are a number of reasons for variants. They include:

> ***1. Eye Skips***: These include misreadings that result in omissions, repetitions, and transpositions of letters, words, and even entire lines.
>
> ***2. Similar Endings or Beginnings***: If the confusion is due to similar endings on two words or lines, so the intervening words are omitted, this error is termed *homoeoteleuton* (similar ending). An English example could look like this:
>
> Yesterday I went to <u>the mall</u>
wearing only my pajamas.
This seemed to irritate the
people working at <u>the mall</u>
security desk.[37]
>
> If a copyist was distracted, it would be quite possible for the copy to jump from the first to the third line, leaving out the phrase in the middle. If it is the case of omission due to a similar beginning, it is termed *homoeoarcton*.
>
> ***3. Mishearing***: If a book was being dictated, it would be inevitable that a scribe would

mishear things. Such a situation appears to have arisen in Romans 5:1. In that verse, the difference of one letter in the Greek word creates the translation "we have peace" or "let us have peace." Regardless of which spelling was original, the main interpretation does not change.

4. Poor Judgment: A copyist might misinterpret the abbreviations that were often used in manuscripts. This was especially true with the name of Jesus, where there are sometimes manuscript variations between "Jesus," "Jesus Christ," "Christ," and "Christ Jesus."

5. Added Instructions: Liturgical instructions also may have been added in some cases, via a "footnote" to further explain a verse, and this footnote later became a part of a number of future manuscripts. Looking at the earliest manuscripts helps scholars determine when this type of variant has occurred.

6. Deliberate Changes: While skeptics argue many such changes, those that have been identified clearly stand out due to the massive number of copies for comparison. In other words, if a change was intentionally made, the other copies that had *not* been changed would show which one was inaccurate.

8. What do you think of the quote from *Misquoting Jesus* that claims, ". . . in some instances, the very

meaning of the text is at stake"? Does this sound reasonable to you? Why or why not?

9. Some people argue that because the Bible writers were prophets, apostles, or followers of Jesus, that there is significant bias in their writings. What is your reaction to this claim?

What the Writers Claimed

The authors of the New Testament books claimed that they were eyewitnesses and reporters of eyewitness events during their lifetimes. Note what the following verses mention regarding the personal involvement of the writers:

> *We did not follow cleverly invented stories when we told you about the power and coming of our Lord Jesus Christ, but we were eyewitnesses of his majesty.* (2 Peter 1:16 [the apostle Peter])

> *That which was from the beginning, which we have heard, which we have seen with our eyes, which we have looked at and our hands have touched—this we proclaim concerning the Word of life.* (1 John 1:1 [the apostle John])

> *For what I received I passed on to you as of first importance: that Christ died for*

our sins according to the Scriptures, that he was buried, that he was raised on the third day according to the Scriptures, and that he appeared to Peter, and then to the Twelve. After that, he appeared to more than five hundred of the brothers at the same time, most of whom are still living, though some have fallen asleep. Then he appeared to James, then to all the apostles, and last of all he appeared to me also, as to one abnormally born. (1 Corinthians 15:3–8 [the apostle Paul])

10. Why are these personal claims important for understanding these books?

11. Since these authors claimed to be eyewitnesses or had contact with eyewitnesses, do you think they have a legitimate motive to help other people learn and understand the facts about Jesus? Why or why not?

What Now?

12. What information in this session has been the most helpful in providing evidence to you that the Bible has been accurately handed down to us today?

13. Which portion of this session do you think would be the most helpful for you in discussing the accuracy of the Bible with someone else?

14. What evidence do you still seek in the process of investigating the claims regarding the Bible?

Consider This

Answer the following belief statements based on your discussion in this session:

15. I believe the Bible has been accurately transmitted from its original copies:
    ___ True
    ___ False
    ___ Not sure

16. I believe there is sufficient evidence that the Bible is an accurate historical description of the events and teachings it provides:
    ___ True
    ___ False
    ___ Not sure

17. I believe the Bible is without error in its originals and is God's inspired, inerrant Word:
    ___ True
    ___ False
    ___ Not sure

18. I believe that the Bible's teachings are of vital importance to my life and the lives of others:
    ___ True
    ___ False
    ___ Not sure

19. Having completed this series, I would like to do the following (Mark all that apply.):
    ___ Become a follower of Christ.
    ___ Recommit my life to Christ.
    ___ Begin a regular time of Bible reading and study.
    ___ Continue with another title in the Contenders series.
    ___ Lead a similar study with some of my friends, coworkers, classmates, or family.

End your final session in a brief time of silent prayer regarding your next step in your spiritual journey. Afterwards, decide as a group what to do next to continue your spiritual growth.

Also, don't forget to look at the "Additional Resources" section for audio, videos, internet materials, and books on this issue that can be used personally or as additional group-learning tools. In addition, we have provided two appendices for your reference. The first is for those who would like to begin a relationship with God. The second is an outline of Bible verses to help you in praying for other people who have yet to experience the joy of a personal relationship with Christ.

Finally, please have a representative from your group take a moment to send an email via the Contenders series website (www.contendersseries.com) to share highlights from your group with others. We would appreciate any stories of life-change that can be used to encourage others in their spiritual journey. God bless you as you continue growing in your spiritual journey!

APPENDIX A:

How to Begin a Personal Relationship with God

If you would like to begin a personal relationship with God that promises joy, forgiveness, and eternal life, you can do so right now by doing the following:

1. Believe that God exists and that He sent His Son Jesus Christ in human form to Earth (John 3:16; Romans 10:9).
2. Accept God's free gift of new life through the death and resurrection of God's only son, Jesus Christ (Ephesians 2:8–9).
3. Commit to following God's plan for your life (1 Peter 1:21–23; Ephesians 2:1–7).
4. Determine to make Jesus Christ the ultimate leader and final authority of your life (Matthew 7:21–27; 1 John 4:15).

There is no magic formula or special prayer to begin your relationship with God. However, the following prayer is one that can be used to accept God's free gift of salvation through Jesus Christ by faith:

> "Dear Lord Jesus, I admit that I have sinned. I know I cannot save myself. Thank You for dying on the cross and taking my place. I believe that Your death was for me and receive Your sacrifice on my behalf. I transfer all of my trust from myself and turn all of my desires over to You. I open the door of my life to You and by faith receive You as my Savior and Lord, making You the ultimate Leader of my life. Thank You for forgiving my sins and giving me eternal life. Amen."

If you have made this decision, congratulations! You have just made the greatest commitment of your life. As a new follower of Jesus, you will have many questions, and this group is a great place to begin. Let your group leaders know about your decision and ask what resources they have available to assist you in your new spiritual adventure.

Other ways you can grow in your new relationship with God include:

- spending regular time in prayer and Bible reading.
- finding a Bible-teaching church where you can grow with other followers of Christ.
- seeking opportunities to tell others about Jesus through acts of service and everyday conversations.

For more information on growing in your relationship with God, please see www.contendersseries.com or www.johnankerberg.org. You can also receive additional materials by contacting the authors at:

The Ankerberg Theological Research Institute
P.O. Box 8977
Chattanooga, TN 37414
Phone: (423) 892-7722

APPENDIX B:

Praying for Those Who Do Not Believe

The Scriptures provide several ways for us to pray for those who do not know Jesus. However, it's often a daunting task to choose where to begin in praying for others. The following outline of verses is designed to assist in offering biblical prayers for those who do not believe.

1. Pray for God to draw the person to Himself.

   No one can come to me unless the Father who sent me draws him. (John 6:44)

2. Pray that the person would desire God.

   But in their distress they turned to the LORD, the God of Israel, and sought him, and he was found by them. (2 Chronicles 15:4)

   God did this so that men would seek him and perhaps reach out for him and find him, though he is not far from each one of us. (Acts 17:27)

3. Pray for an understanding and acceptance of God's Word.

   Consequently, faith comes from hearing the message, and the message is heard through the word of Christ. (Romans 10:17)

   And we also thank God continually because, when you received the word of God, which you heard from us, you accepted it not as the word of men, but as it actually is, the word of God, which is at work in you who believe. (1 Thessalonians 2:13)

4. Pray that Satan would not blind them.

   When anyone hears the message about the kingdom and does not understand it, the evil one comes and snatches away what was sown in his heart. (Matthew 13:19)

   The god of this age has blinded the minds of unbelievers, so that they cannot see the light of the gospel of the glory of Christ, who is the image of God. (2 Corinthians 4:4)

5. Pray that the Holy Spirit would convict of sin.

   When he comes, he will convict the world of guilt in regard to sin and righteousness and judgment. (Matthew 16:8)

6. Pray for someone to share Christ with them.

   Ask the Lord of the harvest, therefore, to send out workers into his harvest field. (Matthew 9:38)

7. Pray that God provides His grace and repentance. (Repentance is a change of mind that leads to changed behavior.)

Repent, then, and turn to God, so that your sins may be wiped out, that times of refreshing may come from the Lord. (Acts 3:19)

For it is by grace you have been saved, through faith—and this not from yourselves, it is the gift of God—not by works, so that no one can boast. (Ephesians 2:8–9)

8. Pray that they believe and entrust themselves in Jesus as Savior.

   Yet to all who received him, to those who believed in his name, he gave the right to become children of God. (John 1:12)

   I tell you the truth, whoever hears my word and believes him who sent me has eternal life and will not be condemned; he has crossed over from death to life. (John 5:24)

9. Pray that they confess Jesus as Lord.

   That if you confess with your mouth, "Jesus is Lord," and believe in your heart that God raised him from the dead, you will be saved. For it is with your heart that you believe and are justified, and it is with your mouth that you confess and are saved. (Romans 10:9–10)

10. Pray that they continue to grow spiritually and learn how to surrender all to follow Jesus.

    Then Jesus said to his disciples, "If anyone would come after me, he must deny himself and take up his cross and follow me." (Matthew 16:24)

    "But whatever was to my profit I now consider loss for the sake of Christ. What is more, I consider

everything a loss compared to the surpassing greatness of knowing Christ Jesus my Lord, for whose sake I have lost all things. I consider them rubbish, that I may gain Christ. (Philippians 3:7–8)

So then, just as you received Christ Jesus as Lord, continue to live in him, rooted and built up in him, strengthened in the faith as you were taught, and overflowing with thankfulness. (Colossians 2:6–7)

Additional Resources

Interested in learning more? For those seriously pursuing more on the life of Christ and Christianity, several additional quality tools exist. We have listed below several other resources available from The Ankerberg Theological Research Institute along with a list of helpful websites on the subject.

Ankerberg Theological Research Institute Resources

All of the following Ankerberg resources can be ordered online at www.johnankerberg.org or by phone at (423) 892-7722.

Books

All of the following books are authored or coauthored by Dr. John Ankerberg or Dillon Burroughs:

Ready with An Answer for the Tough Questions About God (Eugene, OR: Harvest House, 1997).

The Case for Jesus the Messiah: Incredible Prophecies that Prove God Exists (Chattanooga, TN: Ankerberg Theological Research Institute, 1989).

Defending Your Faith (Chattanooga, TN: AMG Publishers, 2007).

Fast Facts on Defending Your Faith (Eugene, OR: Harvest House, 2002).

The Facts on Why You Can Believe the Bible (Eugene, OR: Harvest House, 2004).

Knowing the Truth About the Reliability of the Bible (Eugene, OR: Harvest House, 1997).

Video and Audio Programs & Transcripts

The following topics are available in VHS & DVD format. Most programs offer downloadable transcripts as well.

Answers to Assumed Errors in the Old Testament

Dramatic Archaeological Discoveries That Demonstrate the Reliability of the Old Testament

Evangelicals Debate Biblical Inerrancy

How Was the Old Testament Written?

How You Can Know the Bible is the Word of God

Is the New Testament Historically Reliable?

What Does "The Bible is Inspired and Inerrant" Mean?

Online Articles

Over 2,500 online articles on Christianity and comparative religions are hosted on The Ankerberg Theological Research Institute website. For an A to Z directory, see http://www.johnankerberg.org/Articles/archives-ap.htm.

About the Authors

Dr. John Ankerberg is host of the award-winning apologetics TV and radio program *The John Ankerberg Show*, which is broadcast in more than 185 countries. Founder and president of the Ankerberg Theological Research Institute, John has authored more than sixty books, including the bestselling *Facts On* apologetics series, with over 2 million copies in print, and *Defending Your Faith* (AMG Publishers). His training includes three earned degrees: a Master of Arts in church history and the philosophy of Christian thought, a Master of Divinity from Trinity Evangelical Divinity School, and a Doctor of Ministry from Luther Rice Seminary. For more information, see www.johnankerberg.org.

Dillon Burroughs is a research associate for the Ankerberg Theological Research Institute. Author or coauthor of numerous books, including *Defending Your Faith* (AMG Publishers), *What's the Big Deal About Jesus?*, and *Comparing Christianity with World Religions*, Dillon is a graduate of Dallas Theological Seminary and lives in Tennessee with his wife, Deborah, and two children.

Endnotes

1 These guidelines adapted from Judson Poling, *How Reliable Is the Bible?*, rev. ed., (Grand Rapids, MI: Zondervan, 2003), pp. 14–15.

2 "The Bible and Jesus Myth," *American Atheists*. Accessed at http://www.atheists.org/christianity/myth.html.

3 Adapted from Andrew E. Hill, *Baker's Handbook of Bible Lists* (Grand Rapids, MI: Baker Books, 1981).

4 Kurt Aland, *The Problem of the New Testament Canon* (London: Mowbray, 1962), p. 18.

5 The following section is adapted from Dr. Ron Rhodes, "Crash Goes The Da Vinci Code," http://www.ankerberg.com/Articles/historical-Jesus/DaVinci/HJ-davinci-crash-davinci-code.htm.

6 Cited in Josh McDowell and Don Stewart, *Understanding the Cults* (San Bernardino, CA: Here's Life Publishers, 1982), p. 28.

7 Cited in Josh McDowell and Don Stewart, *Understanding the Occult* (San Bernardino, CA: Here's Life Publishers, 1982), p. 38.

8 Ibid, p. 58.

9 "Some Well-Known Miracles of Jesus," *Bible Resource Center.* Accessed online at http://www.bibleresourcecenter.org/vsItemDisplay.dsp&objectID=F38BB037-BFF6-47FE-A828BEA35B562AE8&method=display.

10 This chart was adapted from four sources: 1) *Christian Apologetics*, by Norman Geisler, (Grand Rapids, MI: Baker Academic, 1988), p. 307; 2) the article "Archaeology and History Attest to the Reliability of the Bible," by Richard M. Fales, in *The Evidence Bible*, compiled by Ray Comfort (Gainesville, FL: Bridge-Logos Publishers, 2001), p. 163; 3) *A Ready Defense*, by Josh McDowell (Nashville, TN:

Nelson Reference, 1992), p. 45; and 4) the online article "Manuscript Evidence for Superior New Testament Reliability," by the Christian Apologetics and Research Ministry. Accessed at http://www.carm.org/evidence/textualevidence.htm#2.

11 Bruce M. Metzger, *The Text of the New Testament: Its Transmission, Corruption and Restoration* (New York: Oxford University Press, 1968), p. 86.

12 From *Origen De Principiis*, Book 2, Chapter 6.4.

13 "Discerning Fact from Fiction in *The Da Vinci Code*." Accessed at http://www.evidenceandanswers.org.

14 Craig L. Blomberg, Ph.D., Review of *The Da Vinci Code* in *Denver Journal, An Online Review of Current Biblical and Theological Studies,* http://www.denverseminary.edu/dj/articles2004/0200/0202.php.

15 Gary Habermas, *The Historical Jesus* (Joplin, MO: College Press, 1996), p. 250.

16 Moses Hadas, "Introduction" to *The Complete Works of Tacitus* (New York: Random House, 1942), pp. IX, XIII–XIV.

17 Ibid, 15.44.

18 Suetonius, *Claudius*, 25.

19 Suetonius, *Nero*, 16.

20 This section adapted from Ralph O. Muncaster, *Examining the Evidence* (Eugene, OR: Harvest House, 2004), pp. 491–494.

21 John Wenham, *The Easter Enigma* (Eugene, OR: Wipf & Stock Publishers, 2005).

22 Cited in the article by John Ankerberg, "If Jesus Wasn't God, Then He Deserved An Oscar," Part 3. Accessed at http://www.johnankerberg.org/Articles/apologetics/AP0701W3.htm.

23 Norman Geisler, *Baker Encyclopedia of Christian Apologetics* (Grand Rapids, MI: Baker, 1998), p. 93.

24 Norman Geisler and William Nix, *A General Introduction to the Bible* (Chicago, IL: Moody, 1978), p. 134.

25 Paul Feinberg, in *Inerrancy*, edited by Norman Geisler (Grand Rapids, MI: Zondervan, 1980), p. 294.

26 James M. Boice, *Does Inerrancy Matter?* (Wheaton, IL: Tyndale House Publishers, 1980), p. 15.

27 This section on inerrancy is adapted from John Ankerberg and John Weldon, "Biblical Inerrancy—part 3," Ankerberg Theological Research Institute, July, 1999. Accessed at http://www.johnankerberg.org/Articles/_PDFArchives/theological-dictionary/TD3W0799.pdf.

28 George Sweeting, *Today in the Word* (Chicago, IL: Moody Publishing, 1989), p. 40. Cited at http://www.bible.org/illus.asp?topic_id=1190.

29 Pat Zukeran, "The Uniqueness of Jesus," *Leadership University*. Accessed online at http://www.leaderu.com/orgs/probe/docs/unique.html.

30 Frederick Kenyon, *The Bible and Archaeology* (NY & London, 1940), p. 288–289.

31 2 Peter 3:16. Some also narrow the number of influences involved to seven if Paul is accepted as the author of Hebrews and the Gospel of Mark is accepted as only an extension of Peter. Interestingly, all nine sources fall into one of three categories—the Apostle, the brothers of Jesus, and the Apostle Paul.

32 Norman Geisler, "The Canonicity of the Bible—Part Two," *ATRI*. Accessed at http://www.johnankerberg.org/Articles/_PDFArchives/theological-dictionary/TD3W0402.pdf.

33 Some figures cited are as high as 200,000. We have used the most common number cited in the literature.

34 Adapted from Ron Rhodes, "Manuscript Support for the Bible's Reliability." Accessed at http://home.earthlink.net/~ronrhodes/Manuscript.html.

35 As cited in Ravi Zacharias and Norman Geisler, general editors, *Who Made God?* (Grand Rapids, MI: Zondervan, 2003), p. 126.

36 Bart Ehrman, *Misquoting Jesus* (San Francisco, CA: HarperCollins, 2005), p. 208. For an evangelical response, see *Misquotes in Misquoting Jesus* by Dillon Burroughs or *Reinventing Jesus* by J. Ed Komoszewski, M. James Sawyer, and Daniel B. Wallace.

37 Thanks to http://www.everything2.com/index.pl?node=homoeoteleuton for this English example.